Praise for *The New Jewish Wedding*

"In a thoughtful and sensitive reworking of her wonderful guide to Jewish marriage, Anita Diamant shows us, once again, that her finger is firmly on the pulse of American Judaism in all its aspects. Inclusive, accessible, and enjoyable to read, Diamant's work now offers an expanded, updated treatment of the questions all Jews ask when they marry: from the rabbi to the reception to the reality of life afterwards. If you are a couple with wedding plans, the parent of a bride or groom, or simply a person interested in delving into the subtle beauty of our tradition, it is hard to imagine a better book than this to accompany you on your journey."
—Rabbi Aaron D. Panken, Dean,
Hebrew Union College-Jewish Institute of Religion, New York

"I am very impressed by this book—by the air of openness and spirituality that pervades its pages. It's a 'how-to' book of the highest quality, for in essence it teaches us how to prepare for and experience the loveliness and sanctity of one of life's most glorious moments: the wedding."
—Chaim Potok

"This is a special book, the product of excellent research, spiritual sensitivity, and the author's genuine empathy for the reader. It is complete, informative, and thoroughly enlightening. Instead of giving directions, it gently provides options. It makes me envy anyone who is planning a wedding. I wish it had existed when my wife and I were planning ours."—William Novak, coauthor of *Iacocca*

"This book glows with love of Judaism."—Susannah Heschel, editor of *On Being a Jewish Feminist*

THE NEW
JEWISH
WEDDING

Revised and Updated

ANITA DIAMANT

A FIRESIDE BOOK   Published by Simon & Schuster
New York London Toronto Sydney

FIRESIDE
Rockefeller Center
1230 Avenue of the Americas
New York, NY 10020

FIRESIDE and colophon are registered trademarks
of Simon & Schuster, Inc.

Designed by Bonni Leon-Berman

Manufactured in the United States of America

7   9   10   8

Library of Congress Cataloging-in-Publication Data
Diamant, Anita.
The new Jewish wedding / Anita Diamant.—Rev. and updated.
p.   cm.
"A Fireside book."
Includes bibliographical references and index.
1. Marriage customs and rites, Jewish.   I. Title.
BM713.D53   2001
296.4'44—dc21   00-049502

ISBN 0-7432-0255-4 (trade pbk.)

The author gratefully acknowledges permission to reprint the following works:

Translation of the Seven Wedding Blessings, by Janet Berkenfield. Reprinted by permission of Janet Berkenfield. Copyright © 2000 by Janet Berkenfield.

Permissions continued on page 271

ACKNOWLEDGMENTS

Two people were crucial to the creation of this book. In addition to being my beloved and my friend, Jim Ball was also my research staff, my copy editor, my proofreader, my cheerleader, and my hand-holder. This is very much *our* book. Nor would you be reading these words were it not for Rabbi Lawrence Kushner, who, when I asked him what I should read in preparation for our wedding, wheeled around from the bookshelf behind his desk, pointed a finger at me and said, "You should write a book about Jewish weddings." From that point on, Larry acted as official godfather to this endeavor. He was (after Jim) the first reader of every chapter. His contributions were invaluable. His influence is pervasive. He has been a great teacher.

While working on this book I found many wonderful teachers who were generous with their time and knowledge. They fed me lunch, challenged my assumptions, and shared their concerns and insights in addition to their expertise. Thanks are due Penina Adelman, Michele Alperin and Steven Sherriff, Rabbi Rebecca Trachtenberg Alpert, Rabbi Ramie Arian, Rabbi Al Axelrad, Rabbi Nina Beth Cardin (who assisted me in consulting the files of the Jewish Women's Resource Center, National Council of Jewish Women, New York Section), Debra Cash, Pattie Chase, Howard Cooper, Lev Friedman, Rabbi Everett Gendler, Rabbi Stuart Geller, Rabbi Burt Jacobson, Joshua Jacobson, Cherie Kohler-Fox, Jonathan Kremer, Cantor Riki Lippitz, Billy Mencow, Peggy McMahon, Larry Moulter, Rosie Rosenzwieg, Reb Zalman Schachter-Shalomi, Rabbi John Schechter, Rabbi Drorah Setel, Rabbi Daniel Shevitz, Rabbi Jeffrey Summit, Ella Taylor, Rabbi Max Ticktin, Rabbi Moshe Waldoks, and Rabbi Arthur Waskow.

Thanks to Arthur Samuelson, for seeing *The New Jewish Wedding* into being in the first place, and to Marcela Landres, for her enthusiastic support for an updated edition.

While preparing this edition of the book, I was fortunate to receive assistance from Rachel Adler, Ari Davidow, Rabbi Lisa Edwards, Rabbi Laura Geller, Rabbi Leigh Lerner, Rabbi Carl Perkins, Rabbi Noa Kushner, Rabbi Sharon Kleinbaum, Rabbi Michael Lezak, Rabbi Joel Sisenwine, and Rabbi Liza Stern.

Finally, thank you to Rabbi Barbara Penzner. Barbara was one of the first people I interviewed for the first edition of *The New Jewish Wedding*. Since then, she has been a resource, sounding board, first reader, commentator, and editor for every one of the Jewish guidebooks I have written since then. She is also one of my most precious friends.

to Jim

my beloved, my friend

CONTENTS

Contents

Contents

11

PART FOUR
CREATING A JEWISH HOME
207

The main function of observance is not in imposing a discipline but in keeping us spiritually perceptive. Judaism is not interested in automatons.

Abraham Joshua Heschel,
Between God and Man

THE NEW
JEWISH
WEDDING

Preface to the
NEW EDITION

There were many reasons to revise and update *The New Jewish Wedding.*
Some are fairly obvious: "Action for Soviet Jewry" is now "Action for
Post-Soviet Jewry"; the list of artists and addresses was outdated long
ago; there is certainly no need to explain the use of the pronoun "she" as
applied to the noun "rabbi" anymore.

The New Jewish Wedding was first published in 1985 as a *minhag*
book—a description of contemporary customs. Customs have changed:
in 1985, klezmer music was still viewed as an exercise in nostalgia and it
could be difficult finding a local calligrapher to write a *ketubah.* Today,
klezmer is hot and Internet *ketubah* boutiques make it possible to hire a
calligrapher anywhere in the world. Today, Jews routinely donate three
percent of the food costs at weddings to Mazon, A Jewish Response to
Hunger, a national non-profit agency that provides food to hungry people of all faiths.

In 1985, the majority of non-Orthodox Jews in North America—the
vast majority—were unaware of the rich trove of traditions, and texts,
and customs that had been lost, forgotten, and abandoned for more than
a generation. At the start of the twenty-first century, most Jewish couples
know that weddings don't have to look like a scene out of *Goodbye,
Columbus* or *Fiddler on the Roof,* or the high-WASP *Father of the Bride.*
Because what was vaguely experimental in 1985 is now mainstream.
Today, the Jewish wedding is a great example of the vitality and dy-
namism of a living Jewish culture, sparkling with fresh artistic expression, spiritual authenticity, and joy.

This edition of *The New Jewish Wedding* chronicles these happy devel-
opments, with creative new translations of the seven wedding blessings,
new *ketubah* texts, poetry, and art. Online resources are featured wherever possible. The addition of a new section called "New Faces under the
Canopy," acknowledges changes in the demographics of the Jewish

world, which has brought many new Jews, non-Jews, and same-sex couples under the *huppah.* While it is beyond the scope of *The New Jewish Wedding* to explore the larger debates about conversion, intermarriage, and homosexuality, no description of contemporary Jewish wedding customs can ignore these changes.

The New Jewish Wedding remains, however, a *minhag* book, a book of choices. Your choices. I hope this edition will be a source of inspiration, discovery, challenge, and joy as you plan your wedding. I pray that you and your beloved share many years filled with inspiration, discovery, challenge, happiness, and peace.

Anita Diamant
26 Nissan 5760
May 1, 2000

FROM THE AUTHOR

It was going to be my second wedding, and I thought it would be a small affair—a few family members in the rabbi's study and then a demure little party for twenty or thirty people in the spacious home of a friend. But it was Jim's first wedding, and his guest list alone included more than thirty people. Besides, "demure" is not the kind of wedding that our rabbi, Lawrence Kushner, went in for.

I remember that what finally sold me on the idea of having a "real" Jewish wedding was Rabbi Kushner's description of *yichud,* a very ancient custom. After the ceremony, the bride and groom spend ten or fifteen minutes together in a room by themselves; no receiving-line crush of well-wishers, just a little time to sit down in peace and look at each other, to share some food and relax before the party to follow. I had no idea that this simple, reasonable, and to me quite wonderful custom was part of Jewish wedding tradition. I wanted to know more.

The more I learned, the more I wanted to incorporate into our wedding ceremony and celebration. Jim and I were married under a *huppah*—a marriage canopy—in the sanctuary at Congregation Beth El of the Sudbury River Valley, surrounded by one hundred loving faces. Neither of us—or any of our guests—had ever attended any wedding quite like ours. The ceremony felt both very old and entirely our own. It was simultaneously very serious and giddily joyous, sentimental but also thought-provoking. It's hard to describe. You had to be there.

The spirit of the ceremony carried over into the celebration afterward. Everyone danced and ate, and our guests entertained us with songs and jokes, cheers, poems, and magic tricks; we all laughed until our sides ached in spite of the unseasonably hot weather. No one had a better time than Jim and me, yet in the weeks following the wedding we actually received thank-you notes from guests!

We were very fortunate to have found Larry Kushner, whose imagination and skill were the primary resources for planning our wedding, because the books that were available to help brides (not couples, mind you, just brides) plan Jewish weddings had more to say about place cards than about *yichud.* The books written by rabbis were full of directions about what is and isn't "correct" according to their particular interpretations of Jewish law.

What Jim and I could have used was a book that would not only supply us with the theological and historical background we needed to understand traditional Jewish wedding practices, but also invite our exploration of and participation in the tradition. And while we weren't interested in doing things Emily Post's way, we still needed some practical advice about such things as composing an invitation and planning a party for a hundred people. There was no such book, which is why I wrote this one.

According to Jewish law and custom, you remain a bride and groom for a full year after the wedding. I wrote *The New Jewish Wedding* as a bride during the year after our wedding, when my need for this wedding book was still very fresh. I read everything I could get my hands on that had to do with Jewish weddings; I interviewed rabbis and talked to recently married couples.

During that year, when acquaintances asked what I was doing and I told them "I'm writing a book about Jewish weddings," the most common reaction was laughter. "It's a humor book, right?" they said, immediately associating the words "Jewish wedding" with the orgy of conspicuous consumption portrayed in the film version of *Goodbye, Columbus.* That Technicolor parody was one of two dominant images of the Jewish wedding in America. The other comes from *Fiddler on the Roof,* with its vague, sanitized portrayal of customs that were quaint but foreign to most American Jews. Given these models, it's no wonder that Jewish weddings became virtually indistinguishable from Protestant weddings.

My wedding had little in common with either of those celluloid fabrications. It was an authentic expression of Jewish life and modern life. It was old and new. It was glorious in every way.

Jim and I signed a *ketubah,* a marriage contract that has been part of Jewish weddings since the first century. But unlike the traditional Aramaic document, with its description of the bride's trousseau and mention of only the groom's marital responsibilities, ours was an egalitarian contract that spells out in Hebrew and English our mutual commitments and obligations. I walked down the aisle side by side with Jim, who had chosen to become a Jew, Yacov ben Avraham v'Sara—Jacob, son of Abraham and Sarah, the first Jews. Our *huppah* was made of Jim's beautiful, new blue-striped prayer shawl, my wedding gift to him, which was held aloft by four cherished friends—two Jews and two non-Jews, two women and two men. Rabbi Kushner chanted the ceremony both in Hebrew and in English. *Yichud,* in a dim classroom down a corridor from the commotion, was just what I'd expected: a magical relief, a moment of truth, an island of peace in a gloriously hectic day.

In Judaism there is a willingness to ignore the boundaries between everyday life and holiness. Thus your wedding begins when you first announce your decision to marry and includes every aspect of planning and preparing for the big day. Even arguments about who gets invited and what gets served for dinner are part of the festivities. Nor is your wedding over until the last thank-you note is written, the last photograph is pasted in the scrapbook, and the last bill is paid. If you are reading this book as a bride or groom, these words are part of your wedding.

I hope you will find this book useful and that you will enjoy reading and sharing it. And I hope that your wedding is everything you want it to be.

Mazel tov!

Anita Diamant

INTRODUCTION

There is no such thing as a "generic" Jewish wedding—no matter what the rabbi tells you, no matter what your mother tells you, no matter what the caterer tells you.

The rabbis who codified Jewish law, *halakhah,** made it so easy for couples to marry that the minimal requirements for carrying out a kosher Jewish wedding can be summed up in a few words: the bride accepts an object worth more than a dime from the groom, the groom recites a ritual formula of acquisition and consecration, and these two actions must be witnessed. That constitutes a Jewish wedding; the rest of the traditions associated with Jewish weddings—the canopy, the seven wedding blessings, the breaking of a glass, even the presence of a rabbi—are customs. Custom—in Hebrew, *minhag*—changes over time and differs from one nation to the next. Some Jewish wedding customs have been discarded and forgotten, and some persist with even greater symbolic and emotional power than the religious prescriptions.

Customs change to meet the needs and express the concerns of people in different eras and situations. Over the centuries the Jewish wedding has been celebrated with countless variations in ritual and *minhag*. It is a dynamic and flexible tradition, and it is yours to explore and recreate.

"To be a Jew in the twentieth century is to be offered a gift," wrote the poet Muriel Rukeyser. Many non-Orthodox Jews tend to believe that this gift belongs really and authentically only to traditionalists. This is simply not true. Orthodox Jews have no lock on Judaism, and this book documents how liberal Jews have been inspired by old practices—the *ketubah*, for example—to create new forms of piety and celebration.

* *The New Jewish Wedding* contains a number of transliterated rather than translated Hebrew and Yiddish words, because their meaning does not survive simple translation into English. Don't be intimidated even if you know neither language! All non-English words are defined and explained at least once in the text, and a glossary appears at the end of the book.

The New Jewish Wedding contains references to biblical, Talmudic, *ha-lakhic,* and mystical texts, stories, as well as prayers, poems, and descriptions of ways creative Jews celebrate marriage in the 21st century. All this is offered as a resource for people who are interested in exploring Judaism's mythic, historic, religious, gastronomic, musical, and literary "gifts" to discover what the tradition offers them today, here and now, at this threshold in their lives.

This is *not* a wedding etiquette book. Etiquette books are rather like insurance policies against doing things "wrong." They presume to instruct you in the "right" way, with the implied warning that if you do not follow the conventions properly you'll be committing terribly embarrassing mistakes. *The New Jewish Wedding* is a *minhag* book that describes the customs and rituals that American Jews are reviving and reinventing to express themselves within a four-thousand-year-old tradition.* Furthermore, this book assumes that both partners care about what happens at their wedding, so it is addressed to both members of the couple—not just to the bride.

The New Jewish Wedding is organized to help you become the architect of your own Jewish wedding. The first section, "Making the Tradition Your Own," lays the foundation for the many choices—some big and some little—you are about to make. It puts your wedding in context, which includes not only Jewish history, theology, and generations-old custom but also the concerns of modern life. Every marriage is a merger of individuals and families, and every merger creates friction. Accommodating both modern sensibilities and a four-thousand-year-old system of beliefs creates even more friction. Transforming that heat into light is the challenge of making Jewish tradition your own.

The section called "New Faces under the Canopy" responds to changes in the demographics of American Jewry, including an unprece-

---

* While I have attempted to include customs from the cultures of Sephardic (Spanish and Mediterranean) and Mizrachi (Middle Eastern) Jews, the *minhagim* in this book tend to reflect the fact that the majority of American Jews are descended from Eastern European ancestors (Ashkenazic).

dented number of converts to Judaism, the fact that nearly half of Jews marry non-Jews, and the increasingly active and open participation of gay and lesbian Jews in communal and ritual life.

The second section, "Ways and Means," will help you transform your ideas and fantasies (and worries and disagreements) into a wedding. It includes descriptions of the all-important tools and props and players that go into making a Jewish wedding and the party that follows: from finding a rabbi and wording the invitation to organizing a processional and hiring a caterer.

The third section, "Celebrations and Rituals," describes the full round of parties and practices that constitute a Jewish wedding. There are customs to mark every stage of the making of a marriage—before, during, and after the "main event" under the *huppah*.

The most important difference between what you hold in your hands and a wedding etiquette book is that *The New Jewish Wedding* pays more attention to the marriage ceremony than to the wedding reception. Although Judaism places great value on celebrating, weddings are considered much more than pretexts for partying. Marriage is foremost a holy obligation—a *mitzvah*—required of every Jew. For the Jewish religious imagination, the wedding has been an allegorical emblem for peak moments of sacred experience: both the covenant at Sinai and the joy of Shabbat are described in terms of the relationship between bride and groom.

The whole wedding liturgy fills no more than a page or two. The few hundred words of the ceremony are very old, their meaning and power compressed into a dense mass, like ancient rocks striated with signs of life from a thousand generations. But custom has created a context for and given *tam*—flavor—to this almost austere ritual. Before the wedding ceremony begins,* guests are welcomed at a *kabbalat panim*—literally "receiving faces." Traditionally, this consists of two separate ceremonies:

---

*Please do not read this précis as *the* recipe for making the definitive Jewish wedding. It is only a brief description of *a* wedding, here only to familiarize you with the complement of Jewish wedding traditions that will be explained later.

male guests go to a *chossen's tish*—groom's table—and women "attend the bride" in another room at a *hakhnassat kallah*. At some point before the *bedeken*—the "veiling" of the bride by the groom—which is attended by all the guests, the *ketubah*—marriage contract—is signed.

The wedding ceremony takes place beneath a *huppah*—a canopy supported by four poles. The liturgy is brief. First there is an invocation, followed by *birkat erusin*—the blessings of betrothal—which include blessing and drinking from the first cup of wine. Then comes the giving and accepting of a ring, accompanied by a brief declaration of consecration called the *haray aht*. Next the *ketubah* is read aloud, the rabbi speaks to the couple, and additional prayers are offered. Then there is the chanting of *sheva b'rachot*—seven marriage blessings—which include blessing and drinking from the second cup of wine. Finally, a glass is shattered, marking the end of the ceremony. The couple then goes to *yichud*—seclusion—for ten or fifteen minutes after the ceremony. Here they break the day-long fast that is customary for brides and grooms.

And somehow, in the heart of the ritual, custom is forgotten. Time collapses. Details like the hour, the date, the style of the bride's dress, the music—all vanish. Somehow it is the wedding of the first bride and groom, when—according to an old story—God braided Eve's hair and stood with Adam as his witness, when God pronounced the blessings and the angels shouted *mazel tov*. During these moments every wedding is the first and also the ultimate wedding in a four-thousand-year-old golden chain.

The last part of the book, "Creating a Jewish Home," touches on some of the happily and not so happily ever after aspects of Jewish weddings, including the traditional week of postwedding celebration.

There have always been many Judaisms. Even before the destruction of the Temple in Jerusalem in 70 C.E.,* Judaism was not a monolithic religion. *The New Jewish Wedding* is an expression of Jewish pluralism. As

---

* C.E., or "Common Era," is a designation that does not refer to the divinity of Jesus, as does A.D., "Anno Domini, the year of the Lord." Similarly, B.C.E. means "before the Common Era."

such, I hope it will be of use to Jews of many different backgrounds, affiliations, and beliefs, which means everyone who reads this book will probably find at least one personally irritating interpretation of Jewish law or custom.

When this happens to you, think of this blessing, which the Talmud provides for the occasion of seeing an audience composed of Jews:

Blessed are you, Adonai our God, Sovereign of the Universe,* who discerns secrets, for the mind of each is different from the other as is the face of each different from the other.[1]

This is the blessing over our diversity.

There is a story told in the name of Rabbi Nachman of Bratslav, a seventeenth-century Hasidic master:

> *A group of people who have been to a wedding are on their way home. One says, "It was a beautiful wedding. I liked the food." Another says, "It was a great wedding. The music was marvelous." Still another one says, "It was the best wedding I ever went to. I saw all my good friends there and we had a terrific time." Rabbi Nachman, who has overheard them, says, "Those people weren't really at a wedding."*
>
> *Then another wedding guest joins this group and says, "Baruch HaShem! [Blessed be the Name!] Thank God those two got together!" At that Rabbi Nachman says, "Now, that person was at a wedding!"*

At the heart of this book is the wish that everyone who attends your wedding—family and friends, witnesses and guests, even bride and groom—will go home talking about the good food and the good time, *and* the fact that you two found each other and decided to invoke the blessings of family, friends, community, and tradition on your love.

* The words "Baruch ata Adonai Eloheynu Melech Ha-olam" introduce every Jewish blessing. The familiar English translation for the Hebrew is "Blessed art Thou, Lord our God, King of the Universe." Several alternative English versions for this Hebrew formula appear throughout this book.

PART ONE

MAKING THE TRADITION YOUR OWN

DECISIONS, DECISIONS

When most Jews lived in small, tight-knit, intradependent communities, a wedding was a wedding: you made it as lavish and invited as many people as you could afford, but the content and meaning of the ceremony were clearly defined by Jewish tradition. The rest of it—the processional, the menu, and such—was determined by local custom. No one needed a book such as this one because people understood themselves in terms of those shared customs and traditions.

For most American Jews, however, weddings are no longer a straightforward expression of shared beliefs and practices. Tradition is not a primary force in our lives. Our communities are scattered and vague. The words of the wedding ceremony lack solid moorings, and our celebrations are mounted by paid professionals. This state of affairs occasions a lot of wailing and breast-beating. But it has also given Jews the opportunity to rediscover and reinvent the Jewish wedding so that it can become a mirror in which people see their own needs and dreams reflected.

Jewish traditions and rituals are not always immediately accessible; you have to learn how to "read" them. To understand the power and beauty of the Jewish wedding, it's important to learn something about its place in Jewish theology, law, history, and custom. This is not an academic or nostalgic process, however. It is a way to find your own roots and grow your own wings.

Rituals dry up and die if they reside only in the library. Judaism is a living tradition because it has been examined, debated, and reinvented, generation after generation. So while Jewish weddings are, by definition, grounded in the past, they are also the stuff of the irrepressible present.

This means that Jews of the twenty-first century cannot marry the same way as their parents did, much less their great-grandparents. The world has changed too much. Our expectations of marriage are not the same. We are different kinds of Jews. Our Jewish weddings synthesize the sum total of our experience, which includes both ancient memories and the headlines in the morning papers.

To make a wedding that is both recognizably Jewish and personally meaningful requires a level of conscious decision making that would have mystified our great-grandparents. Should we use Hebrew words in the wedding invitation? How do we walk down the aisle? What do we want to say to each other under the *huppah*? If we do *yichud,* how can we have a receiving line? How are we going to make this wedding Jewish? How Jewish are we going to make this wedding?

The more numerous the choices, the greater the likelihood of disagreements and conflict between brides and grooms, among families, between tradition and personal style. There's a Yiddish saying, "No *ketubah* was ever signed without an argument." The result of all this learning, choosing, and even arguing is much more than a glorious party. As rites of passage, weddings clarify and express a great deal about the people under the *huppah.* A wedding is a public announcement and demonstration of who you are as a couple. When you draw on Jewish tradition—borrowing, revising, even rejecting, in essence struggling to create meaning with it—the tradition becomes yours.

The Tradition of Marriage

The first of the 613 *mitzvot* (commandments) in the Torah is "Pe'ru ur-vu" ("Be fruitful and multiply"). Judaism sanctifies every dimension of human experience—from birth to death, from eating to eliminating. Sexuality and procreation are sanctified by marriage, the primary purpose of which is the creation of new life. Every wedding sets the stage for the next generation of "the children of Israel." The Talmud records that "one who does not participate in 'be fruitful and multiply' causes God's presence to vanish."[1] Indeed, marriage is seen as the prototypical act of creation. The Zohar, the great book of Jewish mysticism, states: "God creates new worlds constantly. In what way? By causing marriages to take place."[2]

In the Midrash, the imaginative rabbinic literature "somewhere between commentary and fantasy ... that sprouts up in the spaces between the consecrated words of Scripture,"[3] the creation of male and female inspired a fabulous tale about the first wedding.

> *The wedding of the first couple was celebrated with pomp never repeated in the whole course of history. God, before presenting Eve to Adam, attired and adorned her as a bride.... The angels surrounded the marriage canopy, and God pronounced the blessings upon the bridal couple, as the* hazzan *does under the* huppah. *The angels then danced and played musical instruments for Adam and Eve in the ten bridal chambers of gold, pearls and precious stones that God had prepared for them.[4]*

The ongoing work of making marriages is considered so vital that heaven is imagined as constantly astir with news of them. According to the Talmud, "Forty days before the formation of a child, a voice proclaims in heaven: 'So-and-so's daughter is to marry so-and-so's son.' "[5]

The Midrash portrays God as a perpetual *shadchan*, or matchmaker, for the whole world:

> *Once a Roman matron asked Rabbi Jose bar Halafta: "How long did it take the Holy One, blessed be He, to create the world?"*
> *He said to her, "Six days."*
> *"From then until now what has He been doing?"*
> *"The Holy One, blessed be He, is occupied in making marriages."*
> *"And is that His occupation?" the woman asked. "Even I can do*

that. I have many men slaves and women slaves and in one short hour I can marry them off."

"Though it may appear easy in your eyes," he said, "yet every marriage is as difficult for the Holy One, blessed be He, as the dividing of the Sea of Reeds." Then Rabbi Jose left her and went on his way.

What did the matron do? She took a thousand men slaves and a thousand women slaves, placed them in two rows and said, "This one should wed that one, and this one should wed that one." In one night she married them all. The next day they came before her—one with a wounded head, one with a bruised eye, another with a fractured arm, and one with a broken foot.

"What is the matter with you?" she asked.

Each one said, "I do not want the one you gave me."

Immediately the woman sent for Rabbi Jose bar Halafta and said to him: "Rabbi, your Torah is true, beautiful, and praiseworthy."

"Indeed a suitable match may seem easy to make, yet God considers it as difficult a task as dividing the Sea of Reeds," Rabbi Jose acknowledged.[6]

Nor does God disappear once a match is made. According to the Midrash, Adam was first called *esh*—fire, and Eve was also called *esh*. But when they married, two of the letters of God's name *(Yud-Hay-Vav-Hay)* were added to each of theirs. Adam's name became *aleph-Yud-shin, ish*—man, and Eve's name became *aleph-shin-Hay, ishah*—woman. Thus when God's presence is absent from a marriage, there is only *esh* and *esh*, "fire consuming fire."[7]

Although the rabbis considered marriage divine in origin and a holy obligation, they also understood that, as a human enterprise, it was subject to great difficulties and even failure. Keeping God's name in a marriage is no easy task, so the Talmud devotes great attention to the rights and responsibilities of brides and grooms, wives and husbands. The laws regarding marriage cover everything from dowries to sexual conduct to divorce; they are complex, rigorous, often contradictory, and, like much of *halakhah* (Jewish law), undeniably patriarchal.

The commandment to marry is directed toward men. According to the Talmud, a wife can save a young man from "sinful thoughts,"[8] and "Any man who has no wife is not a man."[9] Marriage to a good woman is often described as the source of happiness and blessing for a man. (The Talmud seems generally less concerned with women's happiness.)

Still, *halakhah* was undisputably progressive for its time in establishing certain rights for women: minor girls may not be betrothed, and women have the legal right to refuse any suitor, no matter what their parents command. Although only men can grant divorces, women are entitled to sue for divorce on some grounds, including sexual incompatibility. Conjugal rape is explicitly prohibited in the Talmud. And despite the fact that wives are "acquired" in much the same manner as property, men are required to treat them with respect and tenderness or risk God's wrath.

While Jewish law regulated marriage, Jewish weddings inspired the dreams, prayers, and creative energies of hundreds of generations. "Be fruitful and multiply" is not only God's wish, it is the articulate cry of a people with a precarious place in the world. Among survivors of the Holocaust there is a saying: "To dance at a Jewish wedding is to dance on Hitler's grave." For every generation, weddings are a glimpse into the future, a repudiation of past griefs, and a celebration of the here and now.

In Judaism's pantheon of folk characters, the *shadchan* (matchmaker) is one of the stars. During the Middle Ages, matchmakers were learned men and rabbis, but by the eighteenth century the profession had changed, and they tended to be fast-talking used-car-salesman types who glossed over physical defects and large discrepancies in age with theatrical flourishes of rhetoric. Even so, because the work was considered so important, the matchmaker remained a beloved rogue, so according to the Yiddish proverb, "God does not punish the *shadchan* for telling lies." The profession finally withered away in Europe during the Enlightenment, when the idea of romantic love as a legitimate basis for marriage swept the Jewish world, inspiring dread among traditionalists, who predicted that this change surely presaged the imminent death of Judaism itself.

Modern Life

For most Jews today marriage is no longer so much a commandment as it is an option. While Judaism places an absolute value on marriage, Jews are part of a secular culture in which marriage is no longer necessary to fulfill a man's or a woman's financial, social, or sexual needs. In America today the dividing line between adults and children is not marriage and the establishment of a family so much as it is work and the launching of a career. And even Jewish marriages, which once seemed immune to the divorce epidemic, now have at best a one-in-three chance of lasting for a lifetime.

American Jews tend to marry and have children later than their parents did. Even remaining single is no longer the shame nor the rare exception it once was. Even so, an overwhelming majority of Jews do exercise their option—and perform the *mitzvah*—by marrying.

However, the *mitzvah* of marriage and the ritual of the Jewish wedding have been profoundly transformed by feminism. The legal foundation of the wedding—in which the bride is "acquired" by the groom in a blatant property transfer—is utterly unacceptable to most Jewish brides and grooms. And while Jewish law continues to insist upon the ritual transaction, in practice, the Jewish community has rejected the notion of *kinyan* (acquisition) in favor of *brit,* a sacred covenant between equal partners.

This change is expressed in many ways. For example, the *ketubah,* the Jewish marriage contract, has been completely reimagined. In the traditional language of the *ketubah,* there is no mention of love, or mutual respect, or even God; only the groom's fiduciary responsibilities are spelled out. But the *ketubot* signed by most couples today, do speak of love, as well as respect and reciprocal responsibilities. The contemporary reconstruction of the *ketubah,* which ranges from the addition of one paragraph to total revision, creates room for personal relevance and meaning even as it connects us to our most ancient past.[10]

Jewish women marry under canopies that are made of their own prayer shawls; female rabbis and scholars officiate at weddings; women sign *ketubot* as witnesses and chant the seven wedding blessings for their sons and daughters. Even in more traditional communities where some of these practices are considered radical, women are vocal, visible participants in weddings, in which only a generation ago they were permitted no active role.

Making Jewish Choices

One of the first choices for two Jews planning a wedding today is whether to make the event recognizably Jewish at all. "Do we go to a justice of the peace and forget about religion and tradition altogether?" If the answer to that question is no, you are confronted with a myriad of choices about how to make it a Jewish wedding, which for most people means finding a rabbi, who not only officiates but guides and advises couples about the Jewish content of their weddings. Thus it becomes important to make a good *shidduch*—a good match—with a rabbi. The best matches are those that encourage exploration, discussion, and enough self-confidence so you can make some Jewish decisions for yourselves.*

* See the section "Choosing a Rabbi" for a full discussion of how to find and work with a compatible teacher.

Making choices about the Jewish aspects of your wedding is part of the process of establishing a Jewish marriage and a Jewish home. Since every marriage is a blending of two separate "cultures," it's very common for seemingly uncontroversial discussions—like about how much Hebrew to put on the invitation, or about the relative importance of hiring a kosher caterer—to lead to debates and even debacles. And this is true not only when Jews from different backgrounds get together; it happens even when both members of a couple attended a similar synagogue, religious school, and youth group.

We tend to value and perpetuate those parts of the tradition that most closely coincide with our own lifestyles.[11] For most of us, "traditional Judaism" is what we learned at our parents' knees—without understanding that every family, every synagogue, every Jewish community makes choices. To minimize the conflicts and create more room for compromise, it helps to remember that every Jewish family's way of doing things is only one expression of Judaism. Respecting Jewish pluralism makes it easier for you to make your wedding into a synthesis and avoid the pitched battles.

Anticipating Conflict

All weddings create stress, even if you are respectful of differences and knowledgeable of the tradition; even if you have the most supportive rabbi and parents imaginable. Even if you agree about nearly every choice put before you, your wedding will put you both under enormous pressure. Planning a wedding strains everyone's nerves, but a heated argument about who will be marching down the aisle is rarely just the result of working under a deadline. When you and your mother—or you and your beloved—start yelling at each other about the processional, it's safe to assume that you're not really arguing about who's on first.

Weddings are emotionally charged turning points, not only in the lives of the bride and groom but also and especially for their families. A wedding is a rite of passage that signals major life changes and raises issues about intergenerational dependence and independence. But there is often more involved than issues of the losing-a-son, gaining-a-daughter variety. Life-cycle events are embedded in everything else going on in the family.[12] Your wedding may precipitate conflicts about things that don't seem to have very much to do with the event at hand, including old feuds between cousins and even your parents' own marriages.

Such interfamily dynamics get played out during another conflict-prone process—the merger of two families with different histories, customs, and expectations about what a wedding should be. Although many families do their best to minimize tensions with soon-to-be relatives, even minor misunderstandings deserve careful handling. In such an emotionally charged setting, little things tend to get blown out of proportion and can sour relationships for years to come. The more resolution and harmony you can achieve in the months prior to a wedding, the happier the day will be. If things get really out of hand, a meeting with the rabbi or even a family counselor may be a good idea.

Establishing who pays for what is one of the most common causes of inter- and intrafamily conflict. In the past, things were a little more clearcut. In many communities the groom's family assumed all wedding costs; after all, the bride's family was providing the dowry. More recently it's become customary for the bride's parents to assume the entire cost (a kind of latter-day dowry), except for such things as the groom's clothes and other incidentals, which became his family's responsibility. But today, sometimes even last generation's customs don't address current needs.

Couples who have been financially independent for many years often prefer—and sometimes are even better equipped—to pay their own wedding bills. In such cases, parental gifts of money become a way of "dowering" the marriage. It is increasingly common for wedding costs to be shared among two or three parties: the groom's family, the bride's family, and the couple. This may sound fair and equitable in theory, but in practice it's a complicated way to go.

Money is a potent symbol. For many people, giving money is an important way of expressing love. A parent's refusal to pick up the tab for his child's wedding celebration is a powerful statement of disapproval. Likewise, refusing a parent's offer to pay can represent rejection. Money also determines control. It's rare (but not unheard of) for parents to foot the bills without expecting to influence decision making in proportion to their contribution. Those who write the checks generally, and reasonably, want a say in the outcome.

A simple, straightforward way to help minimize some of the more task-oriented family conflicts (which are often the staging ground for issues of control) is for the bride and groom to prepare a few lists before sitting down with the parents. First, draw up a list of "nonnegotiable" items—aspects of the wedding over which you are not prepared to compromise. These will obviously vary from couple to couple and can range from refusal to have anything to do with rented clothing to the content of the *ketubah*. The second list includes things about which you don't feel quite as strongly and which you are willing to compromise—for instance, the wording of your invitation, music for the processional, the menu. Since these negotiations entail give-and-take, this list might include tasks you have every intention of letting your mother "win": floral arrangements, a family dinner before the wedding, accommodations for out-of-town guests, and so forth.

New Faces under the Canopy

The Jewish community is undergoing unprecedented demographic changes. There are more converts to Judaism than at any point in history since the beginning of the Common Era. Jewish families and institutions now include non-Jewish members in growing numbers. Jewish congregations and communities openly embrace the participation of gay and lesbian members as never before in our history. This variegated influx brings new talents and energies into the Jewish world, and with them, unprecedented challenges.

The new faces under the canopy are the source of new kinds of questions. The following pages provide some answers.

Jews-by-choice under the huppah

There are no accurate or reliable statistics for the number or rate of converts to Judaism, however it is clear that Jews-by-choice are a growing part of the community.[13]

Conversion to Judaism is largely a process of study, which is directed by a rabbi. The curriculum for conversion is set by individual rabbis and can take anywhere from six months to two years. In addition to study, Jewish law requires *mikvah* (ritual immersion) for men and women, and ritual circumcision for men. Converts also meet with a *bet din*,[14] a rabbinical court, which usually consists of three rabbis who question the candidate about his/her sincerity and knowledge of Judaism. (People are almost never "failed" since rabbis will not propose unqualified candidates.)

The vast majority of converts find their way to Judaism by falling in love with a Jew. Thus, conversion rituals and weddings commonly take place within months or weeks of each other. While conversion and marriage each deserve their own celebrations, the synergy between them can lead to dizzying heights of happiness—and stress.

When the rabbi officiating at the wedding is also the referring rabbi for conversion to Judaism, the relationship between the couple and rabbi tends to be strong. Your premarital counseling will be a continuation of your conversionary conversations, which should include discussion about issues that may arise in your families—both Jewish and non-Jewish. Your rabbi may suggest strategies for coping with their anxieties. If non-Jewish family members have never been in a synagogue, the rabbi may suggest they come in for a meeting, or attend the *ufruf*—the communal prewedding celebration in the synagogue (see page 147).

Non-Jewish families often need to be reassured that their presence and participation are important. It helps to put both families at ease by explaining what will happen at your wedding. You might want to send a letter or a copy of the wedding booklet to your extended non-Jewish family and friends well in advance of the big day.

As far as the wedding liturgy and ritual are concerned, there is no difference between a wedding of two born Jews and a wedding where the bride or groom (or both) are Jews-by-choice. A Jew-by-choice is a Jew in every sphere of Jewish life, including under the *huppah.*

However, since many elements of the wedding are purely a matter of custom, there are many ways to include and honor the ethnic, cultural, or culinary traditions from a non-Jewish family of origin. Thus, a Jewish bride of Indian birth can be comfortable wearing a colorful sari rather than a white gown at her wedding. (The white gown is a custom that Ashkenazic Jews borrowed from Christian neighbors during the Middle Ages.) Similarly, a Jewish groom of Scottish birth can be married under a canopy made out of his family's tartan, since *huppah* decoration is basically a matter of custom and taste. Music of any variety can be woven into ceremony and celebration and as for the meal: Italian food, Chinese food, soul food—all have been served at Jewish weddings. (Check with your rabbi if you have questions about Jewish dietary laws.)

With the whole round of rituals and customs surrounding Jewish weddings described in this book, you should be able to find ways to feature most of the important people in your life. Some elements, such as reciting Hebrew blessings, are generally limited to Jews, but others are not. The honor of making the first toast or announcing the happy couple after *yichud* is often given to non-Jewish family and friends. Your rabbi will be more than happy to consult with you regarding what is "kosher."

Jews-by-choice should make their preferences known to the rabbi, as well. Since most rabbis make some personal remarks at the wedding, make sure to let him or her know if you want your guests to hear the story of your unique path to the *huppah,* or if you would rather avoid any mention of your conversion at this particular moment in time.

When the bride and groom are already husband and wife

About one-third of non-Jewish spouses in interfaith marriages eventually decide to convert to Judaism.[15] Often, the decision to convert takes place around the time of a major life-cycle event: before the birth of a child, prior to a bar or bat mitzvah, following the death of a parent.[16]

Among liberal Jews, there is no requirement to have a Jewish wedding after conversion, but many couples choose to reaffirm their marriage vows under a *huppah.* These weddings are often intimate, impromptu gatherings in front of the Torah with only a few witnesses present. However, some couples mark the event with ceremony and celebration, choosing from the entire menu of Jewish wedding rituals and customs described in this book. Many couples mark the occasion by buying or commissioning a beautiful *ketubah,* the Jewish marriage license. Certainly the overwhelming weight of Jewish custom is on the side of more: more guests, more celebration, more eating, more gladness, more joy.

Gay and lesbian Jews under the huppah

Perhaps no change in Jewish life is more dramatic than the shift in attitudes toward the presence and participation of gay and lesbian Jews in communal and ritual life. Until recently, Jewish communities were (like the rest of the world), at worst cruel and at best blind to the existence of gay men and lesbians in our midst. However, since the late 1980s, openly gay and lesbian Jews have become rabbis, cantors, educators, synagogue presidents, federation leaders.

Gays and lesbians have also become brides and grooms, convening family and friends to celebrate loving relationships with Jewish ceremonies and *simchas.* Today, many segments of the community affirm these relationships with formal recognition and public expressions of joy.

Some gay and lesbian couples choose to marry without clergy or official community sanction. Since no Jewish wedding requires the participation of a rabbi or cantor, a "do-it-yourself" commitment ceremony can be a perfectly authentic affirmation of Jewish identity and commitment.*

However, many same-sex couples do want a rabbi (and/or cantor) to officiate at their weddings or commitment ceremonies for precisely the same reasons that straight couples do. All life-cycle events function on three levels: personal, familial, and communal. A wedding transforms a private and intimate relationship into something tangible and public. Weddings convene two separate families and transform them both by acknowledging that they are now one extended family. Finally, every wedding invokes the community's blessing and support for the challenges of sharing a life together; every wedding also transforms the community by adding a new household to it.

For same-sex couples, the rabbi's role as community representative can be deeply affirming and help to heal old wounds of exclusion or worse. Furthermore, rabbis who have worked with other gay and lesbian couples can be a great resource not only in planning a ceremony, but especially in dealing with issues particular to same-sex relationships.

Virtually all of the processes and criteria discussed in "Choosing a Rabbi" apply to gay and lesbian couples. Nevertheless, finding a rabbi who is willing to officiate at a same-sex wedding can be a challenge. Generally, this is a word-of-mouth process. Find out if there is a "gay synagogue" in your community, or a temple where lesbians and gay men are comfortable and welcome.

Although the liberal movements vary in their official sanction for or against same-sex ceremonies, it is important to remember that each individual rabbi in the non-Orthodox movements makes his/her own choices. Thus, while the Conservative movement ruled that "commitment ceremonies should not be performed," [17] you may find a Conserva-

---

* Although some couples and rabbis prefer one or the other, or use other terms, such as *Brit Ahavah* (commitment of love), "commitment ceremony" and "wedding" are used interchangeably in this book.

tive rabbi who will, if asked, officiate at one. On the other hand, you may come across a Reform or Reconstructionist rabbi who refuses, even though those movements support officiation; indeed, the Reconstructionist rabbinical manual includes a commitment ceremony. The official position of the Orthodox movements is an unequivocal "no" to any recognition of, or participation at, a same-sex union.

Together with your rabbi, you will begin making choices that are pretty much the same as the choices facing heterosexual couples: How traditional should we make the ceremony? What shall we serve for dinner? Should we write our own *ketubah* text or shop for one we like? Same-sex couples can choose between gender-neutral egalitarian Hebrew and English, or *ketubot* written especially for gay or lesbian couples. See the section on the *ketubah*, and the *Brit Ahuvim* appendix.

But of course, there are profound differences between weddings for gay and straight couples. The most obvious and painful is the fact that gay relationships have no legal standing. Although commitment ceremonies have attained near-normative status in some parts of the Jewish community, same-sex couples do not enjoy fundamental benefits and protections that married heterosexual couples take for granted, such as joint health insurance coverage, inheritance rights, and guardianship of children.[18] Rabbis working with gay and lesbian couples often insist that they execute wills and full medical powers of attorney before agreeing to do the ceremony.[19]

Another area of difference comes in premarital counseling.[20] Gay and lesbian couples certainly benefit from "standard" sessions about setting up a Jewish home, sharing money, and fighting fair, but many same-sex couples need particular kinds of advice, from finding a compatible photographer to mediating with families.

There are cases where parents, siblings, and both extended families are totally supportive and enthusiastic about the wedding. But sometimes one or both families will be hostile and refuse even to acknowledge the arrival of an invitation. Some families that have welcomed their child's partner to family seders and bar mitzvahs may violently object to the idea of a public commitment ceremony. The variations and permutations are endless. A rabbi who has been through this before can provide some perspective and assist you in sorting through the issues. He or she might advise sending a letter to family and friends months in advance of the wedding invitation, just to give people a chance to get used to the idea. Or the rabbi may even suggest that s/he meet with parents.

One of the challenges for gay and lesbian couples is that many have never attended a same-sex ceremony, making it hard to imagine what their ritual could or "should" look like. A rabbi who has officiated at commitment rituals can help, with stories and perhaps a file with a selection of ceremonies. It is also helpful to look at books that contain both photographs and various liturgies.[21]

Same-sex liturgies run a wide gamut. Some are wholly creative rituals based on alternative Jewish and non-Jewish texts, but many follow the basic pattern of the normative wedding liturgy described in Part Three. In addition to making changes that adjust for gender ("loving friends" rather than "bride and groom"), and references to the relationship between Jonathan and David, or Ruth and Naomi, many commitment ceremonies explicitly mention the bittersweet reality of a ritual that is deeply meaningful and yet legally void.

For example, the rabbi might take a moment after concluding the seven wedding blessings to say something like:

> Before drinking from this cup of joy, we acknowledge that our cup is not quite full. We spill out drops of wine in hope that someday this union will be fully recognized as a marriage by the civil authorities with all of the rights and benefits of marriage, and none of the discrimination that faces these brave souls today.
>
> As we raise the cup, we affirm the joy that it does contain, the gifts of this union, the blessings of this love, and the delight of everyone here to celebrate this simcha.[22]

Non-Jews under the huppah

If you opened to this section first, you may feel overwhelmed by unfamiliar choices and confusing reactions. Perhaps you have encountered disappointment, resistance, or even hostility from members of your soon-to-be Jewish family, or others in the Jewish community. In an era when virtually all barriers between Jews and non-Jews have fallen, a cool or surprised response to announcement of your interfaith engagement can feel like a slap in the face. While there is no excuse for rudeness, it helps to understand how your wedding plans fit into the story of the Jewish people.

For most of Jewish history, marriage between Jews and non-Jews was virtually unthinkable. For centuries, it was an illegal act, from the point of view of both Christians and Jews. For Christian authorities, marriage to a Jew could be seen as apostasy—a form of heresy so radical it was sometimes punished by death—not only for the Christian but also for the Jew.

For Jews, marriage outside the faith meant nothing short of the total repudiation of family and identity, as well as religious belief. Jews who married "out" were essentially dead to the community because of the expectation that their children would not be raised as Jews, thus ending that branch of the Jewish family tree.

Intermarriage changed from the rare exception to a commonplace event only recently. Before 1965, only 7 percent of the community was intermarried, but by the start of the twenty-first century, between 30 and 50 percent of North American Jews marry non-Jews each year.[23] Since surveys show that few children of interfaith families ultimately identify themselves as Jews or affiliate with Jewish institutions, many people see this change as a grave threat to the continuation of the Jewish people.

However, dire pronouncements about the "threat of intermarriage" cannot obscure the reality of contemporary Jewish life. Virtually all extended Jewish families include non-Jews, and the fact is that many of those non-Jews have effectively "married in." Non-Jewish spouses are active synagogue members and supporters of Jewish causes and are actively engaged in raising Jewish children, and one-third of the non-Jews who marry Jews ultimately convert to Judaism.[24]

All statistics aside, the big picture obscures the individual needs of every intermarrying couple who seeks to marry with some form of Jewish sanction. You may be facing new and unfamiliar questions about your own spiritual life and religious beliefs, about family life and how to raise children.

The Jewish partner may be wondering: What *does* my Jewishness mean to me? Why do I care so much whether a rabbi officiates?

The non-Jewish partner may be asking: Does my Catholicism (or Unitarianism) still mean anything to me? Why is my partner, who never goes to temple, suddenly so adamant about having a Jewish ceremony?

It is essential that intermarrying couples get their religious agendas and issues out into the open; this is especially crucial if you also face challenges from family members. No matter who ultimately officiates at the ceremony, many couples benefit from meeting with a rabbi, minister, or priest to help sort through religious differences honestly and respectfully. Some clergy will, after a meeting or phone call, refer you to a discussion group for interfaith couples.

Many intermarrying couples begin their wedding plans by trying to find a rabbi to officiate at their wedding. Although some will officiate at marriages between a Jew and a non-Jew, the majority of rabbis still do not. There are clear denominational differences: Orthodox and Conservative rabbis will not participate. In the Reform and Reconstructionist movements, many individual rabbis will officiate.

In general, rabbis are most interested in working with couples who see Judaism as a primary force in their home and family life. If this is the case for you, make that known to the rabbi in your first conversation. Hearing that the desire for a Jewish officiant comes from you and not from parents makes it far more likely that she or he will want to meet with you.

If, however, the rabbi tells you no, remember that the reasons are not personal. In addition to concerns about Jewish continuity, most rabbis explain that they cannot, in good faith, perform a Jewish ceremony for an interfaith couple because the ceremony only has legal standing for two Jews.

A rabbi (or cantor) does not "marry" any couple; the bride and groom marry each other using the words, *Haray aht m'kudeshet li b'taba'at zu k'dat Moshe v'Yisrael.* "With this ring you are consecrated to me according to the laws of Moses and Israel." The *haray aht* constitutes a formal contract, so if either person is not bound by "the laws of Moses and Israel," the contract is meaningless. Additionally, some rabbis feel that a wedding should reflect both individuals, and that a Jewish ceremony essentially leaves the non-Jew out.

Many rabbis who do not themselves perform intermarriage ceremonies will meet with couples who wish to talk about Jewish choices in their married life. Some will refer couples to a justice of the peace, judge, or another rabbi who does officiate at intermarriages.

Rabbis (and cantors) who do officiate often place certain conditions on their participation. Relatively few rabbis will co-officiate with clergy from another religious tradition, or at ceremonies that take place in a church or include language from the Christian Bible. The rabbi may suggest or even insist that certain parts of the traditional Jewish ceremony be set aside in favor of other readings from the Hebrew Bible, for example, "I am my beloved and my beloved is mine," (from Song of Songs) rather than the *Haray aht.*

Some rabbis require that intermarrying couples agree to take a course on Judaism and/or attend counseling sessions to help clarify religious choices. Others may suggest extra premarital sessions, ask couples to join a synagogue, or even have them sign an agreement promising to raise their children as Jews.

No one should try to force Jewish choices on the non-Jewish partner and, indeed, a good rabbi will help protect against subtle pressure from a Jewish fiancé(e). However, rabbis are unabashed advocates for Jewish living. They may do their best to welcome you into the Jewish community, to encourage Jewish choices, and to foster Jewish continuity in the home you are about to establish.

Most clergy—Christian and Muslim as well as Jewish—believe that children do better in homes where parents pick one tradition or the other for the whole family. For many intermarrying couples, the wedding can be an important milestone on a shared spiritual journey toward fuller Jewish commitment, but this is not the case for everyone. Indeed, premarital counseling with clergy helps some couples clarify their resolve to build a truly interfaith life together, one that honors both Jewish and non-Jewish traditions.[25]

Caveat emptor. It is possible to hire a rabbi willing to co-officiate with a minister or priest, perform a ceremony in a church, and say just about anything you tell him to say. Mercenary rabbis (so-called by disapproving peers) make a great deal of money by selling their services to families who insist on a Jewish wedding for couples who don't much care one way or another. These rabbis (and it should be noted that anyone can call himself or herself a rabbi) rarely require meetings with the couple prior to the wedding. They sometimes advertise in Jewish newspapers offering "life-cycle services" and generally charge much more than the going rate for a wedding.

However, if a serious Jewish presence is important to you, try to find someone who cares enough about you and your future to spend time getting to know you and helping you craft a meaningful ceremony.

Some intermarrying couples decide that a civil ceremony is the best option for them and, indeed, many rabbis suggest it. Having a justice of the peace or a judge officiate may calm family tensions about which religious tradition will "win." And if you really want a ritual that incorporates both your traditions—or only borrows a few words or customs from each—you may be better off crafting your own wedding ritual. Some justices of the peace specialize in helping couples write ceremonies that are true to both traditions.

PART TWO

WAYS AND MEANS

PLANNING
THE WEDDING

CHOOSING A RABBI

The person who reads the wedding blessings at a Jewish wedding is called the *mesader kiddushin,* the one who "orders" the ceremony of *kiddushin,* or sanctification. That person does not "marry" the bride and groom; they marry each other. According to halakhah, a *mesader kiddushin* must be a Jew who is knowledgeable about Jewish laws regarding weddings and marriage. Thus, it is not necessary for a member of the clergy—rabbi or cantor—to officiate at a wedding for the event to be kosher and binding. From a Jewish perspective, nonordained Jewish scholars, educators, and community leaders may officiate. Couples who prefer that their Jewish ceremony be conducted by a family member or friend who is Jewishly knowledgeable but not licensed by the state can have the civil ceremony and documents executed by a judge or justice of the peace.

However, most people do prefer to have a rabbi and/or cantor officiate at their Jewish wedding. And in fact, the weight of custom is very strong in this regard, dating back to Maimonides, the great rabbinic authority of the twelfth century, who advised the Jews of Egypt that marriages required the supervision of an ordained rabbi.[1] And as an official of both the Jewish community and also as an agent of the secular authorities, a rabbi ensures by his participation that the marriage will be recognized as legal by all interested parties—not the least of whom are the families of the bride and groom.

Often there is no question of "choosing" a rabbi. If either or both of you belong to a synagogue, the congregation's rabbi may expect to officiate, and if you are planning a "hometown" wedding, your parents' congregational rabbi—who may or may not be the rabbi of your childhood—may conduct the ceremony. If your best friend happens to be a rabbi *and* you belong to a congregation *and* there's a family rabbi in the picture, the ceremony can be divided among them in any number of ways. Most rabbis are experienced at "sharing" a wedding with colleagues; this can be done easily and gracefully, without giving offense to anyone.

Given the substantial number of Jews who are unaffiliated with any religious institution, couples often find that they have little or no idea of where to begin looking for a rabbi. Childhood images of "the Rabbi" persist far into adulthood, which means that some people are intimidated by, suspicious of, and sometimes even hostile to anyone who bears the title. It's useful to think about selecting a rabbi the same way you go about choosing any other professional whose services you wish to use. If you wouldn't pick a dentist at random, don't try that approach with a rabbi. Ask people whose opinion you trust and/or who are familiar with a particular rabbi; go to see rabbis "in action," officiating at a ritual or leading a worship service. And expect to talk to two or three rabbis before making a decision.

If you are new to a community or want a comprehensive listing of local clergy, get in touch with the national denominational offices. For a Conservative rabbi or cantor contact the United Synagogue of Conservative Judaism, 155 Fifth Avenue, New York, NY 10010, 212-544-7800, www.uscj.org. For a Reconstructionist rabbi, contact the Jewish Reconstructionist Federation, c/o Beit Devora, 7894 Montgomery Avenue, Suite 9, Elkins Park, PA 19027, 215-782-8500. For a Reform rabbi or cantor, contact the Union of American Hebrew Congregations, 633 Third Avenue, New York, NY 10017, 212-650-4000, www.uahc.org.

Generally, people who are interested in having their marriage solemnized by an Orthodox rabbi will already be familiar with the local community, its clergy, and shuls (synagogues.) If, however, you are new to town or want a list of Orthodox* synagogues and rabbis, you can contact the Union of Orthodox Congregations of America, 11 Broadway, New York, NY 10003, 212-563-4000, www.ou.org.

Cities with sizable Jewish populations often publish a directory that is available from the local federation or community center.

If you are in any way affiliated with a university, the campus Hillel rabbi is a logical candidate, since you are already part of his or her "congregation." But unaffiliated Jews sometimes call upon Hillel rabbis with the expectation that people who work with college students are more flexible, liberal, or easier to approach. Although some campus rabbis are more accessible than some congregational rabbis, it is unwise to make too many assumptions about any rabbi's style or theology based on age, gender, or even affiliation, since the lines between movements are increasingly blurred.

Once you have a list of likely candidates, attend a service or lecture, and if you like what you see, approach the rabbi afterward and explain why you're there and that you'd like to make an appointment to discuss your wedding plans. (This is an excellent method of capturing the attention of even the busiest rabbi.)

A few practical considerations can be dispatched over the phone—first of all, there's the question of the rabbi's availability and your wedding date. (If you care about your ceremony, find a compatible rabbi before renting a hall or hiring a caterer.) Both the bride and the groom—and only the bride and groom—should attend meetings with the rabbi. (Mothers are *not* invited, no matter how involved they are in planning the wedding.)

At the initial interview you can expect to be asked about yourselves in some detail: family history and religious background, education, career,

---

* Orthodox Judaism is, itself, a designation that embraces a variety of "Torah-based" approaches. The OU represents what is commonly called "Modern Orthodoxy."

Elana Ruth Taubman
and
Michael Asher Schwartz

25 November 2000

אילנה ומיכאל

ב"ח חשון תשס"א

I AM MY BELOVED'S
& MY BELOVED IS MINE

*Different examples of
wedding invitations.
Top left and right:
© Jonathan Kremer,
right: © Elaine Adler*

We invite you to rejoice
at the wedding of our daughter
Susan Melinda
and
Arie Paul
son of Aubrey and Roleen Katz

Rosh Chodesh Sivan 5759
Sunday, May 16, 1999
at 4:00 P.M.
Rancho Las Lomas
Silverado, California

Melinda and Hall Seely

Mirth and merriment
to follow

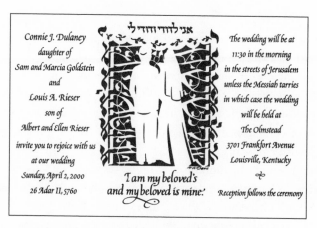

אני לדודי ודודי ל

Connie J. Dulaney
daughter of
Sam and Marcia Goldstein
and
Louis A. Rieser
son of
Albert and Ellen Rieser
invite you to rejoice with us
at our wedding
Sunday, April 2, 2000
26 Adar II, 5760

The wedding will be at
11:30 in the morning
in the streets of Jerusalem
unless the Messiah tarries
in which case the wedding
will be held at
The Olmstead
3701 Frankfort Avenue
Louisville, Kentucky

Reception follows the ceremony

I am my beloved's
and my beloved is mine.

Different examples of wedding invitations.
Top: © Peggy H. Davis, bottom left and right:
© Susan Leviton

You have created joy and gladness, bridegroom and Bride,
love and harmony, peace and companionship.
שמחה, חתן וכלה, אהבה ואחוה ושלום ורעות

Rejoice with us at our wedding

Carol Barbara Selkin & Richard Michael Wise
Daughter of   Son of Ethel
Hortense and   and the late
Bernard Selkin   Milton Wise ל״ז

Sunday, May 16, 1999   1 Sivan 5759

קבלת-פנים Greeting the Bride and Groom
4:00 p.m.
בדקן Veiling the Bride 5:00 p.m.
חופה Marriage Ceremony 5:30 p.m.

The Sheldon Concert Hall & Ballroom
3648 Washington Boulevard, St. Louis

Dinner following the ceremony

I am my beloved's and my beloved is mine
אני לדודי ודודי לי

Rejoice with us
Nancy & Robert Klein   Virginia & William Boockvar
at the wedding of our children

טובה פעריל   בנימין שמעון
Tovah Patricia & Kenneth Stephen

Saturday, December 31, 1994
6:30 P.M.
Hillel Foundation
11291 Euclid Avenue
Cleveland, Ohio

Black Tie Optional

previous marriages, children, and individual and common hopes for your marriage. Few rabbis will be surprised if you mention that you are living together. Even very traditional rabbis will not turn you away on grounds of previous "immorality." While premarital sex and cohabitation are forbidden by Jewish law, neither renders you unfit for marriage. If either of you has been married before, some rabbis will ask about a *get*—a Jewish writ of divorce.*

Before meeting with the rabbi ask yourselves what you want from a rite of passage. What is your preferred style of celebration? How, for instance, do you mark birthdays? With elegant candle-lit dinners or with paper hats and noisemakers or with both? Think about weddings you've been to, weddings you've read about, weddings you've seen in the movies. What did you like about them and what made you uncomfortable?

Have some specific questions ready for your first meeting. You might ask the rabbi to describe the most beautiful wedding he/she ever conducted—what made it special? Although the wedding liturgy is simple and brief, rabbis develop a pattern or sequence they find meaningful and effective, so ask how he/she usually proceeds. Ask how much of the ceremony will be translated into English. If you are sensitive to language that refers to God only in the masculine gender, you should say so, and perhaps ask how he/she translates the phrase "Baruch ata Adonai"—a phrase that is repeated many times during the wedding. Try to determine the rabbi's willingness to incorporate your ideas for personalizing the service; bring up any ideas you may have about poems, songs, or individuals you would like included.

Most rabbis want to get to know the people for whom they act as *mesader kiddushin* and will expect to meet with you a number of times. Most recommend meeting three, four, or five times before the wedding. Given the time pressures on rabbis, however, scheduling these appointments is usually the responsibility of the couple, who are wise to make

* See the section "Divorce."

these sessions a priority since they may be some of the few moments you have to reflect upon the awesome commitment before you.

Rabbis take their role as premarital counselors very seriously and generally want to spend more time talking about your marriage than the wedding. The rabbi might ask you to start this conversation by describing the marriages in your families. Some rabbis ask couples to fill out a questionnaire about their relationship; others suggest keeping a journal in the six months before the wedding, with instructions to note the times that strengthen their relationship and the times that seem to threaten the bond or create distance.

Astute rabbis can be a great resource in negotiating family issues and conflicts that surround virtually every wedding. They have accompanied many couples down this rose-and-thorn-strewn path before and know how to listen, guide, and advise you.

Since the wedding marks the beginning of a Jewish home, the rabbi will want to discuss ways for you to start making Jewish choices together. He or she may ask you to do some reading in advance of a meeting, and then discuss such topics as: observance of Shabbat and the yearly cycle of holidays, the placing of a mezuzah at the door, raising Jewish children, and affiliating with a synagogue.

Some people think of the rabbi as a kind of spiritual chauffeur—someone who simply takes you where you tell him or her to go. Rabbis are understandably put off by couples who approach them with lists of "demands." While it's important to communicate confidence in your own abilities to make Jewish decisions and to be clear about your basic requirements, there are limits to the process of give-and-take.

The rabbi has obligations beyond providing you with help and understanding. He/she also has a responsibility to Jewish tradition as he/she understands and interprets it. There are some things every rabbi feels he/she cannot do or condone and still remain true to his/her understanding of *halakhah*, of the *mitzvot*, of Jewish peoplehood. These vary greatly from one rabbi to the next, but it would be disrespectful, pointless, and self-defeating to insist on something a rabbi cannot, in conscience, go along with.

Fees. Generally, if you are a member of a congregation, the rabbi's services are covered by dues or membership fees. Even then, however, a gift to the rabbi's discretionary fund is appropriate and thoughtful. If you are not members, the rabbi will inform you of his/her fee. If the amount he/she mentions would cause a hardship, most rabbis will do their best to accommodate you. If the wedding will be held out of town, the rabbi should be reimbursed for all expenses.

Some people are outraged that rabbis charge anything at all to preside at weddings. Others think of payment to the rabbi as a sort of tip. Rabbis are professionals whose services are worth compensation. The time they spend meeting with couples and officiating at weddings is time away from family and other responsibilities. Ask when and how payment should be made; the rabbi should never have to send you a bill.

It is customary to invite the rabbi and his/her spouse to the party following your wedding. (The same holds true for cantors and their spouses.) The rabbi and/or cantor should receive an invitation as a courtesy. Be sensitive to his/her observance of the dietary laws; if he/she keeps kosher, platters of shrimp would be an embarrassment for everyone. In the past, the rabbi's presence at a wedding celebration proved the importance of the family. Do not be disappointed, however, if your rabbi declines your invitation or stays at the festivities for only a short time. It's difficult to enjoy a party at which you are acquainted only with the bride and groom, especially since rabbis report that wedding guests often feel compelled to be on their best behavior around any member of the clergy. This could even put a damper on the merriment, which would run contrary to the *mitzvah* of rejoicing with the bride and groom.

Cantors

Cantors are Jewish clergy whose primary job is leading congregations in prayer and song. Cantors frequently co-officiate with a rabbi, but many also act as the sole leader for wedding ceremonies.

A cantor (in Hebrew, *hazzan,* or *hazzanit* for a woman) is trained in Jewish liturgical music, which includes chanting from the Torah and singing life-cycle prayers, such as the beautiful seven wedding blessings. Most states license cantors to perform weddings, and some will meet with couples, as described above, to plan and counsel.

When and Where

Jewish ritual may be characterized as the art of significant forms in time, as architecture of time. *Most of its observances—the Sabbath, the New Moon, the festivals, the Sabbatical and the Jubilee year—depend on a certain hour of the day or season of the year. It is, for example, the evening, morning, or afternoon that brings with it the call to prayer. The main themes of faith lie in the realm of time. We remember the day of the exodus from Egypt, the day when Israel stood at Sinai; and our Messianic hope is the expectation of a day, of the end of days.*

Abraham Joshua Heschel, The Sabbath [2]

You can raise a *huppah* anywhere. Although there are customs and conventions about "appropriate" locations for weddings, just about any place can be made a holy place by human action and intention. Time, however, is another matter. Fully one out of seven days—Shabbat—is forbidden, and there is a list of dates on the Jewish calendar when weddings are proscribed.* Thus weddings are integrated into a yearly cycle during which "Every hour is unique and the only one given at the moment, exclusive and endlessly precious."³

Weddings are forbidden on the Sabbath not only because of the inevitable work and travel that would violate the laws prescribing rest from all labor, but also because of the injunction that every *simcha*—every joy—be celebrated and savored individually. According to Jewish law, "One should not mix rejoicing with rejoicing." The combining of two joys risks that one or both of them will not be given its due, which is why double weddings are discouraged.

Weddings may not be held on the major holidays and festivals, including Rosh Hashanah, Yom Kippur, Passover, Shavuot, and Sukkot. (Hanukkah and Purim are exempt from this prohibition.) In Orthodox and Conservative practice, there are two extended periods of public mourning during which marriages are not solemnized: the three weeks between the seventeenth of Tammuz and the ninth of Av, which generally fall in July and/or August and commemorate the destruction of the Temple, and the Omer period, between Passover and Shavuot, seven weeks that usually fall in April and May. Lag b'Omer, the thirty-third day in the counting of the Omer, is exempt from the prohibition and is a very popular day for weddings in Israel. In all cases, ask your rabbi and consider your family's level of observance before deciding on a summer date. Likewise, the fast days of Tisha b'Av, the tenth of Tevet, the seventeenth of Tammuz, and the fast days of Gedaliah and Esther are not acceptable wedding dates among traditional Jews.

If either the bride or groom becomes a mourner (a designation limited to someone who has lost a parent, child, sibling, or spouse), the wedding should be postponed for at least thirty days following burial. For a parent, the postponement may be even longer. But in general, the *mitzvah*

---

* Jews follow a lunar-solar calendar that uses the moon for its basic calculations. The lunar year generally, but not always, has twelve months, which are not aligned precisely with the solar Gregorian calendar.

of marriage is so important that weddings take precedence over almost everything else, and in some cases may even preempt mourning. Your rabbi will be able to advise you should (God forbid) the situation arise.

Tastes in wedding dates have changed very little over the centuries. In biblical times weddings were commonly scheduled in the spring during the month of Adar, when "the winter is past, the rain is over and gone; the flowers appear on the earth; the time of singing is come and the voice of the turtle is heard in our land" (Song of Songs).* The autumn was also a popular time for weddings; on the fifteenth of Av, a late summer/early fall month, the unmarried girls of ancient Israel would dress in white and go out to sing and dance in the vineyards, where the young men would follow to seek brides.

For many generations the selection of an auspicious wedding date was of the utmost importance, although customs varied over centuries and continents. The Zodiac was often consulted in hopes of invoking good spirits and fooling evil ones. The moon was also shown consideration in setting a date. It was considered prudent to marry on the new moon, the first day of the Jewish month, which is celebrated by the holiday called Rosh Hodesh, or as the moon was waxing in the sky—a symbol of growth and fertility. Some days of the week were associated with good luck, others with bad. Monday was generally avoided because in the Book of Genesis the phrase "and God saw how good this was" does not appear. On the other hand, Tuesday was favored because those words appear twice. The five-day work week made Sunday the most popular day for scheduling weddings. Saturday-night weddings, the most common choice for formal, evening weddings, traditionally begin an hour and a half after sunset, to avoid violation of Shabbat, though some liberal rabbis will start earlier during the long days of summer.

* Song of Songs—in Hebrew, *Shir haShirim*—is a chapter in the Bible composed of a collection of wedding hymns. Also called "The Holy of Holies," these sometimes passionate love poems were interpreted by the rabbis as symbolic of the relationship between God and the people of Israel.

The hour of the ceremony is up to you. The later the wedding, the greater the expectation of formality. If you are early risers, an evening ceremony followed by a party that lasts into the wee hours is probably not what you want. Sometimes, the hour is determined by the kind of food you want to serve, the availability of the place you're using, and other details. As you plan, take into account the different kinds of energy and emotional connotations of the "seasons" of the day: morning/ spring, afternoon/summer, evening/autumn. Or consider choosing a time that the two of you associate with your first meeting or with any important event in your lives together.

There are no laws regarding where a wedding may or may not take place. During the Middle Ages some weddings were even held in cemeteries, since it was believed the life-affirming act of marriage could halt a plague.[4] There are time-honored traditions for holding weddings in the groom's home, in the bride's home, in a social hall or function room, outdoors, and inside a synagogue. Some Orthodox Jews do not marry in a sanctuary, believing that the *huppah,* symbolizing the marital bedroom (among other things), does not belong near the Torah scrolls.

In America today, Jewish weddings are commonly held in synagogues. A sanctuary, especially one in which you have prayed, offers a spirit of *kedusha,* holiness, in which to start a marriage. The synagogue also provides a link with the larger Jewish community. Since many synagogues have complete kitchen and function-room facilities, couples often choose to have the entire celebration under one roof, not only for the sake of convenience but also to maintain the spirit of the wedding ceremony in the festivities that follow.

Although there are no descriptions of wedding ceremonies in the Bible, a *huppah* under the sky harks back to what was probably biblical custom. Outdoor weddings in a synagogue courtyard became very popular in medieval Europe. Ceremonies were often held in the evenings, the stars shining reminders of God's promise to make Abraham's descendants "as numerous as the stars of heaven" (Genesis 22:17). Today outdoor weddings are still popular, with arboretums, parks, rented estates, and backyards among the sites where *huppot* are raised. If your festivities are going to be held at a hotel and you aren't entirely happy with the décor, layout, or *kedusha* of the function room at your disposal, it may be possible to arrange an outdoor ceremony on the grounds. (Since outdoor weddings always add anxiety over weather, decide whether rain is something you want to worry about and make contingency plans for.)

Do not procrastinate about finding and booking a location for your wedding. Some popular facilities must be reserved years in advance, especially if you have your heart set on a date in June or September.

Jewish weddings have been sanctified in boathouses and on barges, in catering halls and on beaches. Wherever you are going to marry, spend some time there alone together. If the wedding is going to be held in a park, pick the exact spot and imagine yourselves under a *huppah,* surrounded by family and friends. If you're going to marry in a synagogue, take a few minutes to sit in the sanctuary sometime when it's empty and quiet. This may seem like an unnecessary errand, but it will help you to savor the upcoming "endlessly precious" hour.

Invitations and Wedding Booklets

For most of Jewish history, weddings were not by-invitation-only events. In the shtetls of Eastern Europe the whole community would be involved in some aspect of the celebration. One went to a wedding (or a *bris,* or a funeral, for that matter) because it was a *mitzvah* to do so—not only for the fun of it but also to fulfill the Talmudic injunction to rejoice with the bride and groom. On Israeli kibbutzim today, the entire community still gathers to celebrate the weddings of its members.

Today in America we invite. We make lists, which never include absolutely everyone we want to invite. The size of the guest list is determined by family obligations, budget, and decisions about the style of the celebration. The final tally is a composite of as many as four lists: the bride's, the groom's, the bride's parents', and the groom's parents'.

Some people try to avoid conflict by setting a fixed numerical limit: the principals invite fifty people each and that's it.

In theory that's fine, but in practice Judy's family numbers in the dozens; and there's no way to avoid offending all of them without sixty-five invitations. Meanwhile Ben's family includes all of six people, and they're going to feel terribly outnumbered. And since Ben and Judy are paying for half of the wedding, they feel entitled to invite their many friends. Obviously, the final list has to be a compromise that minimizes family strife and maximizes happiness—or at least satisfaction.

The form of American Jewish wedding invitations has generally conformed to the dictates of secular etiquette. In many cases the only indication on a wedding invitation that anything Jewish is going on is the location of the ceremony and perhaps a family name.

But a wedding invitation can be more than a formulaic announcement of a date, place, and time. It can give your guests a foretaste of the ceremony you're planning and provide hints about the kind of energy that is expected of them. Abandoning the once de rigueur high-church tone and British spellings, couples can create distinctively Jewish invitations that begin the rejoicing.

Phrasing that departs from standard invitationese is sure to capture guests' imaginations. You needn't be "honoured" to invite people—you can be "pleased" or "happy" or "delighted." Their "participation" might be as important to you as their "presence." You might decide to invite people to "dance at" your wedding rather than just "attend":

Susan Cohen
and
Hal Green
invite you to dance at their wedding
on Sunday, June 15, 2000
at two o'clock
Temple Beth El
Mitzvah, Massachusetts
Please reply

❁

Hanna and James Cohen and Mary and Al Green
invite you to share
in the joy of their children's wedding.
Susan and Hal
will meet under the huppah
on Sunday, May 6, 2000
at two o'clock
Temple Beth El
Mitzvah, Massachusetts

❁

The joy which the two of us,
Susan Cohen and Hal Green,
give to each other,
we wish to share with our family and friends.
Our parents,
James and Hanna Cohen, of New York City,
and
Al and Mary Green, of Orange, New Jersey,
invite you to join us in the simcha of our wedding
on Sunday, May 6, 2000
at two o'clock
Temple Beth El
Mitzvah, Massachusetts

Some couples and families print the entire invitation both in English and Hebrew on facing pages, though the content of each may be quite different. Although Hebrew names, dates, and phrases now appear more frequently on the English "side," there are some unique phrases, common to Hebrew invitation texts, that rarely get translated into English. For example, it is traditional to invite guests to attend the wedding "in the streets of Jerusalem, unless the Messiah tarries, in which case the wedding will be held at Congregation Beth Emmet . . ."

Don't be afraid to use Hebrew. A transliterated word or a few clearly translated words used in the text or the graphic design informs your guests that Jewish tradition will be honored at your wedding. And don't worry about confusing people with the unfamiliar; in general, both non-Jews and Jews are far more intrigued than intimidated by the presence of Jewish elements in an invitation.

Susan Anna   *Harold Joseph*

daughter of   *son of*

James and Hanna Cohen   *Al and Mary Green*

invite you to celebrate the simcha of their marriage

on Sunday, June 4, 2000

1 Sivan 5760

The huppah will be raised at 2 o'clock

Temple Israel

7000 Nachas Road

Smetna, Kansas

To locate your wedding in the flow of Jewish time, you can identify the date on the Jewish calendar either before or after the Gregorian calendar date: "Sunday, June 4, 2000/1 Sivan 5760." If the date falls on the celebration of the new moon: "Sunday, June 4, 2000/Rosh Chodesh Sivan 5760." Another way to situate a wedding in Jewish time is to mention the Torah reading closest to your wedding date: "Saturday, August 19,

Bri'at HaOlam Ketubah
© by Amy Fagin

2000/18 AV 5760, following Shabbat Ekev." For a rather dramatic announcement of the date, a wedding can be described as taking place "5761 years after the creation of the world, Tevet 19." Some Israeli invitations mark time with the phrase "In the 51st year since the creation of the state of Israel."

Finally, recalling the tradition of giving to the poor during times of personal joy and adding to the *mitzvah* of their marriage, some couples add a note requesting that guests make a donation to charity.

> *We feel that even at an occasion as joyous as a wedding we should remember those in need. Therefore, in lieu of a gift to us, we suggest a gift to one of the following:*
>
> *[A list of charities, with addresses, is given.]*
>
> *P.S. We would be delighted to accept poems, prose, amulets, mandalas, your thoughts, reminiscences or prognostications, and any other such mementos of the occasion.*

It is very common to use a biblical passage on wedding invitations. The most familiar quotations come from Song of Songs, including "I am my beloved's and my beloved is mine," and "This is my beloved, this is my friend." Some passages seem especially appropriate for outdoor weddings: "Come my beloved, let us go out to the field," and "You shall go forth in joy and in peace shall you be led. The mountains and hills shall burst into song before you, and all the trees of the field shall applaud." There are also lines that balance male and female imagery: "Like an apple tree among trees of the forest is my beloved among the youths. Like a rose among thorns is my darling among the maidens."

Another common source for quotes is the seven wedding blessings: "You created joy and gladness, bridegroom and bride, mirth and exultation, pleasure and delight"; also "The voice of joy and the voice of gladness."

The Torah portion for the week of your wedding might suggest a phrase for the invitation, or consider a brief passage about marriage from

Eretz Ketubah
© *by Gad Almaliah*

the Talmud or the Zohar, or other Jewish sources.* This story from the
Baal Shem Tov makes a wonderful invitation quotation:

> *From every human being there rises a light that reaches straight
> to heaven. And when two souls that are destined to be together find
> each other, their streams of light flow together, and a single brighter
> light goes forth from their united being.*

* Browse through the wedding poems that begin on page 219 for inspiration.

אני לדודי ודודי לי

I am my beloved's & my beloved is mine

בשבת

שנת ON THE DAY OF THE MONTH OF IN THE YEAR SINCE THE CREATION

חמשת אלפים ושבע מאות

לבריאת OF THE WORLD AS WE RECKON TIME HERE IN

CORRESPONDING

עולם למנין שאנו מונים כאן

TO • IN KEEPING WITH THE TRADITIONS OF MOSES AND ISRAEL-

WE • THE BRIDE • עם החתן

AND THE GROOM • ועם הכלה

עומדים אנו בכל חופה זו אל מול בני משפחה וידידים למחש

STAND UNDER THE HUPPAH BEFORE FAMILY AND FRIENDS TO AFFIRM OUR COMMITMENT

דבר בואנו בברית נישואין כדת משה וישראל • יחדיו נחלוק

TO EACH OTHER: WE SHALL BE LOVING & SUPPORTIVE COMPANIONS—PARTNERS IN MARRIAGE•

בנישואין חיי ידידות ואהבה והינו עזר כנגד זה לזה תמיד ובית

WE WILL ESTABLISH A HOME AMID THE COMMUNITY OF ISRAEL • GUIDED BY REVERENCE

נקים בקהילת בית ישראל אשר יראת השם רוחו ומקדש

FOR THE DIVINE AND SANCTIFIED BY THE TRADITIONS OF OUR PEOPLE • THE SYMBOLS AND

יהיה במסורת עמנו • יהיו ארחות ביתנו ומנהגו מסילה

RITUALS IN OUR HOME WILL FORGE A LINK TO OUR RICH HERITAGE•A BOND STRENGTHENED

למורשת עתירה וגשר ללמידה ולמעורבות במעשים טובים•

BY INVOLVEMENT• LEARNING AND GOOD DEEDS• WE WILL SHARE LIFE'S PLEASURES AND

יחדיו נחלוק האות החיים ומכאוביהם סמוכים באהבתנו זה

SORROWS• SUSTAINED BY OUR LOVE & DEVOTION • MAY WE BE BLESSED TO RAISE CHILDREN

לזו • מי יתן ותהא הברכה שורה בגדול ילדים בביתנו האוהב

IN A LOVING HOME AND INSTILL IN THEM AN APPRECIATION FOR OUR HISTORY & LEGACY•

אשר ייטב לטעת בלבם גדולת יערכי עמנו ומורשתו•

WITH GREAT JOY • WE ENTER INTO THIS COVENANT OF MARRIAGE• IT IS VALID & BINDING•

שמחה היא לנו לבוא בברית הנישואין והכל שריר וקים•

Garland Ketubah
© *by Jonathan Kremer*

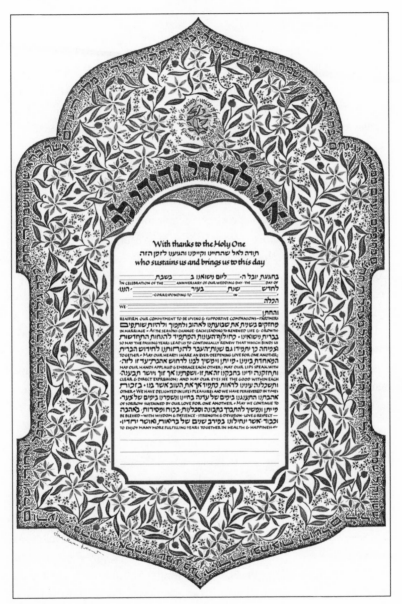

Blessing Ketubah
© *by Jonathan Kremer*

Invitations can be engraved or printed, photocopied or handwritten calligraphically, or composed with the help of a computer. You can hire a calligrapher to write your invitation; however, this is an expensive option and, in fact, not all scribes are willing to take on such small, labor-intensive assignments. Luckily, graphic designers with a good selection of Hebrew computer fonts can provide a wide choice of lettering options and produce a beautiful invitation for the design and paper you select.

To complement the words, you can use the design of your *ketubah* as inspiration, or select symbols from Jewish tradition that appeal to you: menorahs and lions, rings and cups, violins and candles, pomegranates (biblical symbols of plenty), doves (universal symbols of peace). The letters of the Hebrew alphabet can be a source of graceful embellishment. The only Jewish rule that applies to the design of your invitation is *hiddur mitzvah*, the rabbinic call for the beautification of sacred acts. Choose what pleases you.

Invitations should be mailed four to six weeks in advance of the wedding, and the calligrapher may need a few months to finish your order, especially if you plan to marry during his/her busy seasons—early summer and autumn. After the artwork is completed, the printer may require another one to three weeks.

Enclosures. The tongue-in-cheek Yiddish-English "translation" for R.S.V.P. is "Remember to Send Vedding Presents." This formal abbreviation or simply "Please reply" should be sufficient reminder for guests to respond. However, it has become customary to enclose a reply card ("M—— will/will not attend") and a self-addressed, stamped envelope to ensure an answer. (Etiquette mavens decry this development as proof of the laziness of wedding guests, who no longer voluntarily write formal reply notes as in the past.) This adds an additional expense for the hosts. One alternative is to include a self-addressed postcard that says only "Please respond." Not only does this minimize postage costs a bit, but

Song of Songs Ketubah
© *by Mickie Caspi*

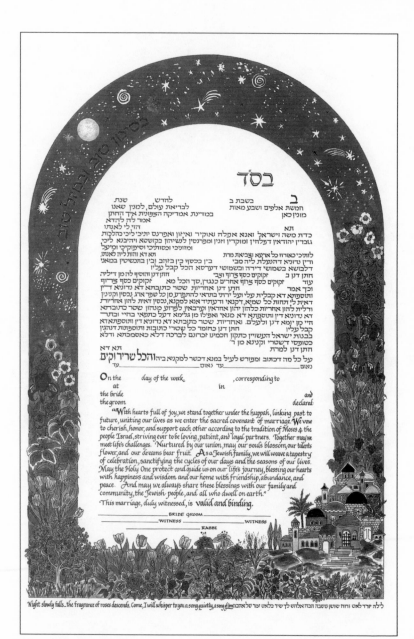

Night Sky Ketubah
© *by Betsy Platkin Teutsch*

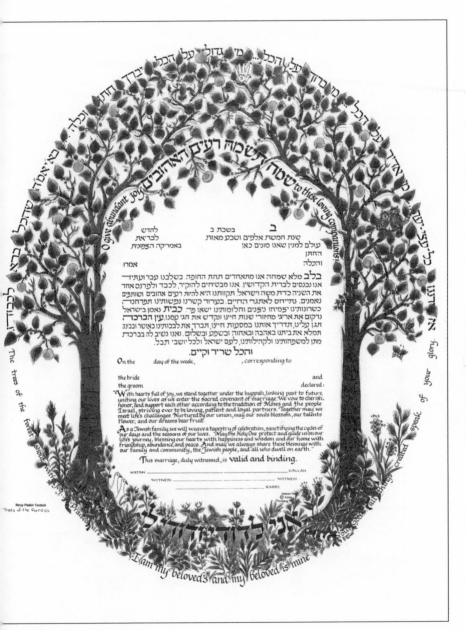

Trees of the Forest Ketubah
© *by Betsy Platkin Teutsch*

Florentine Columns Ketubah
© *by Mickie Caspi*

some of the replies will be priceless and maybe even fuel for the fire of a master of ceremonies.*

Various enclosures may need to be included in the envelope, such as directions to the synagogue, hotel rates, and the like. If there is going to be a special *Oneg Shabbat* (an informal gathering after Friday evening services) or an *ufruf* (recognition of the groom—and bride—by calling them up to the Torah during Shabbat morning services), you might include a photocopied note inviting people to attend. (Family dinners generally don't require a written invitation.) And if you're planning a participatory celebration in which the bride and groom are treated—as tradition dictates—like a queen and king, you can ask your guests to come prepared to entertain you with jokes, reminiscences, magic tricks, poems, juggling routines, songs, dances, and happy hearts.

Wedding Booklets. Couples who reclaim and reinterpret Jewish wedding tradition often find that words and customs that have become second nature to them are unfamiliar to their families and friends. In order to explain and put people at ease, many couples are providing a sort of "program" for their guests—a guidebook to the events of their day.

Wedding booklets can contain everything from your *ketubah* text to acknowledgments of the musicians. Some couples write a letter welcoming their guests and inviting their participation; others include definitions of terms (not everyone knows what a *huppah* is) and explanations of customs such as *yichud*, historical background, and a step-by-step guide to the ceremony.

The booklet can be simple or elaborate. It can consist of a single photocopied sheet of paper or a pamphlet of many pages, bound and printed on glossy paper. It can be typed or written in calligraphy, decorated or plain. For the cover, couples have reproduced the design of their wedding invitation or their *ketubah*. Not only is the booklet a meaningful part of

* See section "Laughter, Music, and Dance."

the day, it serves as a kind of "souvenir" on a much higher spiritual plane than monographed cocktail napkins.

This "new" custom is really only a variation on an old practice. Jewish weddings have long featured a booklet called a *bencher* from the word *benchen,* or prayer. (*Benchen*—or *benching*—refers specifically to praying the *birkhat hamaẓon* after meals.) *Benchers* contain *birkhat hamaẓon,* the blessings after meals, and the seven marriage blessings, which are repeated after eating. (See "Concluding the Festivities" for more on *benching* and *benchers.*)

Wedding Clothes, Wedding Rings

. . . God has dressed me with garments of exultation, . . . As a bridegroom puts on a priestly diadem, And as a bride adorns herself with her jewels.
—Isaiah 61:10

While priestly diadems are rarely part of wedding costumes these days, the attire and adornment of brides and grooms remain as important as in biblical times. The common panic over finding the "perfect" dress or shoes or suit is not merely an exercise in vanity. After all, wedding clothes are the most important ritual garments most of us will ever own. Although the rabbis of the Talmud warned against excessive displays of finery at weddings so as to spare the feelings of poor relatives, the traditional image of the bridal couple as king and queen invites elegance and display.

There are no *halakhic* or legal requirements regarding dress other than the injunction that clothes be both modest and attractive, which leaves a great deal to personal taste and contemporary style. Paintings, drawings, and descriptions of Jewish bridal costumes throughout history demonstrate that Jews have always been influenced by local fashion. While Ashkenazic brides wore the white gown and lacy veil common to European Christian weddings, Sephardic brides donned bright, colorful costumes, their veils often decorated with a cascade of gold coins, similar to the garments of their Muslim neighbors. Grooms' fashions varied similarly.

There is, however, one religious imperative that has too long been neglected, from Minsk to Morocco to Michigan. The *mitzvah*/obligation of rejoicing at a wedding is incumbent on the bride and groom as well as on the guests. Anything that gets in the way of the bride's or groom's happiness—from a too-tight waist to uncomfortable shoes to someone else's idea of "appropriate"—is worse than a nuisance. It's a sin! Whatever you wear, it should make *you* feel attractive, regal, and terrific.

Although Jewish law is quite relaxed about wedding apparel, there are some sartorial customs that have attained the force of law. One of these is the wearing of bridal white. In Jewish practice the wearing of white has as much to do with spiritual purity as physical virginity. A wedding is considered a personal Yom Kippur, a day of repentance and forgiveness for the couple. Among Orthodox Jews the bride's white dress indicates that she has been to the *mikvah,* the ritual bath, in preparation for the wedding, and the groom's *kittel* (a short white linen robe bound by a white belt and worn over his suit) represents his spiritual readiness for marriage.

In traditional practice, a veil is part of the bride's attire as a reminder of Rebekah's action and as a symbol of modesty. (In Genesis, Rebekah "took the veil and covered herself" when she first saw Isaac, her husband-to-be.) The shape and size of the veil match the style of the wedding dress, and a headdress of some sort is customary. The ancient use of crowns to celebrate the "royalty" of the bridal pair is still echoed in the use of a tiara or a floral garland to anchor the veil. Some liberal Jews do not attach much importance to the veil and have dispensed with it. And while some women dislike its associations with Middle Eastern *purdah,* the heavy covering of married women, others claim that the veil is the one piece of clothing that makes them feel set apart and uniquely "bridal."

A groom dons the *kittel* just before entering the *huppah* and removes it after the wedding ceremony is over. *Kittels* can be purchased at Judaica shops or easily made by using a bathrobe pattern or elongating a shirt pattern. The belt should be made of the same material as the garment.[5] Wearing the *kittel* is an Ashkenazic custom. Sephardic grooms sometimes wrap themselves and their brides in a single large *tallit* (prayer shawl) during the wedding ceremony, creating an intimate *huppah* beneath the *huppah.*

While the bride's veil is traditionally worn only once, a *kittel* is worn on special ritual occasions throughout life: on Yom Kippur, at Passover seders, and, finally, as a shroud. Recently some women have turned parts of their wedding attire—a short veil, a white shawl, *tallis,* simple white dress, or even a bridal *kittel*—into ritual garments that are also worn at religiously significant moments, which might include the *brit* (covenant) celebration of a child.

Wedding Rings. In Jewish law a verbal declaration of marriage is not legally binding in and of itself. There must be also an act of *kinyan*—a formal, physical acquisition. Without the groom's giving and the bride's acceptance of some object of nominal value—something *shaveh p'rutah,* literally, "worth a penny"—there is no marriage. Ever since the seventh century, a ring has been the traditional and preferred object of exchange.

According to Jewish law, the ring must be unpierced and free of precious stones to avoid any possible misrepresentation of its value. The ring should belong to the groom, although he may borrow one if the bride is aware he has done so.[6] Only one ring—given by the groom to the bride—is required by law. Believing that an exchange of rings invalidates the *kinyan,* some Orthodox rabbis refuse to perform double-ring ceremonies. Liberal rabbis, however, incorporate the bride's gift of a ring to the groom in the ceremony.

For the most part, Jewish wedding rings are extremely simple pieces of jewelry. Even in the European communities of the sixteenth and seventeenth centuries in Europe, when large, ornate marriage rings decorated with the towers of the Temple in Jerusalem were lent to the bridal couple for their wedding celebrations, a simple ring was later substituted for everyday use.

A band made of a single pure metal, with no holes breaking the circle, represents the wholeness achieved through marriage and a hope for an unbroken union. The circle is an ancient symbol common to many cultures. In various times and places it has been a sign of perfection, completion, safety, and the female. The mystics who wrote the Zohar perceived the ring as a circle of light that revealed the "enveloping" sexual mystery of marriage.[7]

While simple gold bands remain the traditional and most popular choice, embellishment with Hebrew letters has come back into fashion. It was once common for the words *mazel tov*—good luck—to be engraved inside the ring. Some couples choose the declaration. "Dodi Li V' Ani Lo" ("I am my beloved's and my beloved is mine"), which is sometimes rendered in gold filigree on the ring. Jewelers who cater to the Jewish community generally have a selection of rings designed specifically for Jewish weddings. Hebrew names and/or the Jewish date of the wedding can be engraved inside.

The *Ketubah*

To the Midrashic imagination, the whole Torah is a *ketubah*—a marriage contract—between God and the people of Israel. But for American Jews of the past few generations the *ketubah* was often little more than a formality. The rabbi generally supplied a printed document and explained its significance to the bride and groom on the day of the wedding. It would be signed in the rabbi's study or on a corner of a banquet table, sometimes read during the ceremony, and then filed away along with the secular marriage certificate, more or less forgotten. Early Reform rabbis ignored the tradition of the *ketubah* altogether. But the *ketubah* has experienced a major revival and is once again a source of inspiration for artists and calligraphers. For many couples it has become a Jewish focal point in their wedding preparations.

Tradition. The *ketubah* is one of the oldest and one of the least romantic elements of Jewish weddings. It is a legal contract, pure and simple. In its traditional form the *ketubah* does not mention love or trust or the establishment of a Jewish home or even God. It is written in Aramaic, "the technical, legal language of talmudic law, rather than in Hebrew, the language of the Song of Songs."[8]

A traditional *ketubah* is not a contract between bride and groom but a document signed by two witnesses who testify that the groom "acquired" the bride in the prescribed manner and that he agreed to support her. This is not a mutual agreement; the bride only has to willingly accept the groom's proposal of marriage. The *ketubah* is then given to the bride as a surety of her rights and her husband's duties; it becomes her (not their) possession.

The *ketubah* was actually a very progressive document for its time (the end of the first century, C.E.) because it provided women with legal status and rights in marriage. It is also credited with strengthening the Jewish family since it made divorce—otherwise an easily exercised male prerogative—a more costly decision. Since the second century, rabbis held that without a *ketubah* "the union of husband and wife was unhallowed cohabitation,"[9] and it remained a crucial document for many generations. In 1306, when Jews were stripped of their belongings and expelled from France, the rabbinic authorities declared that until new *ketubot* were delivered to the wives, there could be no conjugal relations.[10] However, Jewish law does recognize the validity of marriage without the document. If witnesses testify that a Jewish couple is living together as husband and wife, a *bet din,* a court of rabbis, considers the traditional *ketubah* to be in effect.

While *ketubot* have been written on all kinds of paper and ornamented in countless ways, changes in the text were unusual. Some Sephardic *ketubot* embellished the names of the principals with long lists of honorifics: "... the bridegroom, who bears the good, resplendent name, the perspicacious, the wise, of holy seed, the honorable Abraham, a pure Sephardi, the son of the honorable, who bears a good name, the exalted gentleman, the uplifted one in name and praise, the wise and perspicacious one, of holy seed, the honoured Rabbi and teacher Isaac . . ."[11] During perilous times *ketubot* included special pledges by the groom not to take "adventurous voyages or to expose himself to the risks of travellers and traders."[12]

By and large, however, variations in the *ketubah* were insignificant compared with the extent to which the text remained constant. The document still in use among traditional Jews shares a great deal with marriage contracts from the second century, C.E. (See the Orthodox *ketubah* on page 90.)

New Ketubot.

Although it was a great advance for its time, the traditional *ketubah* does not address the realities of marriage in our day. It is very difficult for many couples and rabbis to use the traditional text and then affirm, as it declares, that the *ketubah* is not to be regarded as an *ashakhta*—"a mere formula." The elaborate economic arrangements for the dissolution of a marriage as spelled out in a traditional *ketubah* have become meaningless, and the changed aspirations, roles, and responsibilities of women and men find no expression in a contract that demands specific duties and responsibilities of the groom but asks the bride for nothing in return.

Since the early 1970s, and especially since the publication of a sample "equalized *ketubah*" in the *First Jewish Catalog,* brides and grooms, rabbis, and calligraphers have been experimenting with new *ketubot.* One rabbi has called these documents *brit ketubot*—"covenant *ketubot*"—an expression that acknowledges the difference between these new contracts and traditional *ketubot* and also emphasizes the seriousness and mutuality of an agreement to marry.[13]

Today, couples have a great variety of published *ketubah* texts from which to choose. And if you don't find one that suits you, you can always

Two Huppah Covers
© *by Jeanette Kuvin Oren*

write your own. If you are concerned with observing "the letter of the law," the traditional text must appear on your *ketubah.* However, it is permissible to add onto the basic document. Indeed, some Orthodox and Conservative rabbis suggest or even require a codicil calling upon the groom to grant his wife a religious divorce (called a *get*) in addition to a civil divorce in case the marriage ends.[14]

New *ketubot* impose many choices on couples, starting with the content of the document. Some brides and grooms use the traditional Aramaic text but select or write an entirely different text in English. Many non-Orthodox couples, uncomfortable with any reference to silver *zuzim* or *kinyan* (ritual acquisition of the bride) in any language, purchase or commission a *ketubah* that reflects their values and hopes in both Hebrew and English. The *ketubah* texts at the end of this chapter will give you some sense of the variety of documents in use today.

One of the most fundamental changes on new *ketubot* is not even what the document says, but who signs it. On the Orthodox document, only two official witnesses sign, and the text reflects this by referring to the bride and groom in the third person. On most new *ketubot,* the couple signs, reflecting the first-person promises they make to each other; then the rabbi and witnesses add their signatures.

It is possible to be both "traditional" and "contemporary" in this regard: Jewish law requires the signature of two observant Jewish male witnesses, but since there is no prohibition against additional signatures, some couples ask two Jewish women to add their names. Some couples invite the entire company to sign. (A large mat surrounding the *ketubah* is one way to accommodate many names.)

Hiddur Mitzvah. Unlike the writing of a Torah scroll or other ritual documents, there are relatively few requirements for the lettering or form of a *ketubah.* But according to the rabbinic principle of *hiddur mitzvah,* when a physical object is needed to fulfill a commandment, the object should be made as beautiful as possible. The *ketubah* has been lovingly and variously interpreted and decorated through the generations.

The earliest known decorated *ketubah* dates from the tenth century, and illustrated and illuminated *ketubot* have been produced by Jews all over the world ever since, in styles reflecting the tastes of nations and epochs. The Jews of Persia made *ketubot* that seem to float on magic Oriental carpets, and North African Jews surrounded the text with the intricate geometrical shapes that also adorned the mosques of their Muslim neighbors. The Italian *ketubot* of the seventeenth and eighteenth centuries are especially elaborate, alive with birds, flowers, signs of the Zodiac, representations of biblical lovers and even pagan gods and goddesses. At the other range of the spectrum, the *ketubot* of poor European Jews who fled pogroms and persecution were often little more than irregularly scrawled letters on coarse brown paper; and the rough documents that survived time and steerage are more emotionally powerful than illuminated Italian masterpieces preserved in museums.

Your rabbi may well be able to provide you with a *ketubah,* usually a document produced by his/her movement. Some of these are quite attractive, and may suit your needs and tastes perfectly. However, many couples enjoy the opportunity of shopping for a text and a design that reflects their tastes.

Modern brides and grooms have an unprecedented choice in selecting both the text and decoration of their *ketubot.* While a simple Hebrew text meticulously lettered on fine parchment can make for a timeless and elegant *ketubah,* color and design can transform the document into a work of fine art. Modern *ketubah* artists employ techniques ranging from paper cutting to lithography, silk-screening to watercolor. The range of design and calligraphic styles is almost dizzying and available to nearly everyone; beautiful *ketubot* are available in such a broad price range, virtually every couple can afford to own something lovely.

Judaica shops and Jewish bookstores carry a good selection of *ketubot* and even more are on view on the World Wide Web. The keyword "ketubah" will lead you to dozens of "galleries," with artists who can provide a choice of texts in Hebrew and English.

Many calligraphers take assignments to create one-of-a-kind *ketubot* as well. These are the most costly and require several months' notice.*

If you are an artist, calligrapher, or simply an avid do-it-yourselfer, you can make your own *ketubah*, and indeed it is considered a great *mitzvah* to do so.

Afterward. According to Jewish law, the *ketubah* becomes the property of the bride after the wedding. In Persia, women kept *ketubot* under their pillows, carefully folded inside silk envelopes. Today, however, many couples frame and hang their *ketubot* in special places in their homes. If you shared the same bed before marriage, hanging the *ketubah* over it affirms the change in your relationship.

The Baal Shem Tov said that if a couple was fighting, they should read the *ketubah* aloud to each other because this would help them remember the day of their marriage, when they affirmed their covenant with each other, when they were surrounded with love and good wishes, and when God entered their relationship.[15]

* The names and addresses of the calligraphers and artists whose works appear in this book may be found on page 239.

Sample *Ketubot*

Orthodox Ketubah

On the ____ day of the week, the ____ day of the month _____ in the year five thousand seven hundred and _____ since the creation of the world according to the reckoning which we are accustomed to use here in the city of _____ in _____. That _____ son of _____ of the family _____ said to this maiden _____ daughter of _____ of the family _____, "Be my wife according to the law of Moses and Israel, and I will cherish, honor, support, and maintain you in accordance with the custom of Jewish husbands, who cherish, honor, support, and maintain their wives faithfully. And I here present you with the marriage gift of virgins, two hundred silver zuzim, which belongs to you, according to the law of Moses and Israel; and I will also give you your food, clothing, and necessities, and live with you as husband and wife according to the universal custom." And _____, this maiden consented and became his wife. The trousseau that she brought to him from her father's house in silver, gold, valuables, clothing, furniture, and bedclothes, all this _____, the bridegroom accepted in the sum of one hundred silver pieces, and _____ the bridegroom consented to increase this amount from his own property with the sum of one hundred silver pieces, making in all two hundred silver pieces. And thus said _____ the bridegroom, "The responsibility of this marriage contract, of this trousseau, and of this additional sum, I take upon myself and my heirs after me, so that they shall be paid from the best part of my property and possessions that I have beneath the whole heaven, that which I now possess or may hereafter acquire. All my property, real and personal, even the shirt from my back, shall be mortgaged to secure the payment of this marriage contract, of the trousseau, and of the addition made to it, during my lifetime and after my death, from the present day and forever." _____ the bridegroom, has taken upon himself the responsibility of this marriage contract, of the trousseau and the addition made to it, according to the restrictive usages of all marriage contracts and the additions to them made for the daughters of Israel, according to the institutions of our sages of blessed memory. It is not to be regarded as an indecisive contractual obligation or as a mere formula of a document. We have followed the legal formality of symbolic delivery (kinyan) between _____ son of _____ and _____ daughter of _____ this maiden and we have used a garment legally fit for the purpose, to strengthen all that is stated above,

AND EVERYTHING IS VALID AND CONFIRMED.

Attested to _____ Witness
Attested to _____ Witness

To transform the Orthodox text into what might be called a "traditional/egalitarian" *ketubah,* some couples add an additional paragraph or two. A *ketubah* may contain agreements above and beyond what is commanded in the Torah, which is the groom's pledge to provide the bride with food and clothing and his pledge of a sum to be paid in case of death or divorce. So it is permissible for the bride to voluntarily assume some responsibilities, or for both bride and groom to add a list of promises or dreams. Some traditionalists prefer to set such additions apart, either by means of calligraphic style, design, or even language, so there is no confusion between what is *halakhicly* prescribed and what is additional. Here is an example:

We have learned by study that the basic principle of Jewish marriage is that husband and wife take equal responsibility for entering into and maintaining their marriage. For it is written (Baba Kama 15a): "Scripture has made man and woman equal with regard to all the Laws of the Torah." Thus when _____, this woman, consented and became his wife, she did so by saying to _____, "I will. And be thou my husband according to the Law of Moses and Israel and I will work for you according to the custom of Jewish wives who work for their husbands, and honor, support, and maintain them in truth. And I will provide your food, clothing, and necessities which belong to you according to the law of Moses and will live with you in conjugal relations according to universal custom. And to this _____, the bridegroom said, "I will."

_____ and _____ each contributed valuable property to the marriage and pledged their spiritual and emotional resources to its maintenance. They exchanged gold rings that each might carry a symbol of this pledge and of their love for each other.

New Ketubot

Egalitarian Ketubah

On the ____ day of the week the ____ day of _____ five thousand seven hundred _____ since the creation of the world as we reckon time here in _____

The bride _____ daughter of _____ and _____ promised _____ the groom, son of _____ and _____. You are my husband according to the tradition of Moses and Israel. I shall cherish you and honor you as is customary among the daughters of Israel who have cherished and honored their husbands in faithfulness and in integrity.

The groom _____ son of _____ and _____ promised _____ the bride, daughter of _____ and _____. You are my wife according to the tradition of Moses and Israel. I shall cherish you and honor you as is customary among the sons of Israel who have cherished and honored their wives in faithfulness and in integrity.

The groom and bride have also promised each other to strive throughout their lives together to achieve an openness which will enable them to share their thoughts, their feelings, and their experiences.

To be sensitive at all times to each others' needs, to attain mutual intellectual, emotional, physical, and spiritual fulfillment. To work for the perpetuation of Judaism and of the Jewish people in their home, in their family life, and in their communal endeavors.

This marriage has been authorized also by the civil authorities of
_____ .

It is valid and binding.

Witness _____   Witness _____
        _____   _____
Bride   _____   Groom   _____
Rabbi   _____

This *ketubah,* written by Rabbi Bernard H. Mehlman, Rabbi Gustav Buchdahl, and Rabbi Eugene R. Lipman and widely circulated throughout the 1970s, has served as a model for countless marriage contracts. Rabbi Lawrence Kushner, wrote and designed its innovative and much-copied two-column format.[16]

Alternative Egalitarian Ketubah Text

On the ___ day of the week, the ___ day of the month of _____, in the year 57 _____, corresponding to the ___ day of _____ in the year 2___ here in _____, the beloveds, _____ and _____ entered into this mutual covenant as equal partners, loving and supportive companions in life.

These rings symbolize our commitment to each other as beloved and friends before God and these witnesses. We shall treasure and respect each other with honor and integrity as we create a loving future together. May our love provide us with the determination to be ourselves and the courage to pursue our chosen path. With this ceremony we affirm our intention to provide for each other the protections and privileges of all loving couples. May our lives be intertwined forever and be as one in tenderness and devotion.

As we share life's everyday experiences, we promise to strive for an intimacy that will enable us to express our innermost thoughts and feelings; to be sensitive at all times to each other's needs; to share life's joys and to comfort each other through life's sorrows; to challenge each other to achieve intellectual and physical fulfillment as well as spiritual and emotional tranquility.

We also promise to establish a home amid the community of Israel, committed to the creation of an all-inclusive society; a loving environment dedicated to peace, hope and respect for all people; a family filled with love and learning, goodness and generosity, comfort and compassion.

We joyfully enter into this covenant and solemnly accept its obligations. All this is valid and binding.

© Mickie Caspi and Caspi Cards & Art

A New Ketubah Text

On the ____ day after Shabbat, the ____ day of the month of _____, in the year five thousand seven hundred and _____ since the creation of the world, as we customarily count time, in _____, United States of America.

How the groom _____ son of _____ said to the bride _____ daughter of _____: *I have found the one that my soul loves.* Be a wife to me in accordance with the law of Moses and Israel. And I will work for you and honor you and nourish you and support you in the ways of Jewish men who work for and honor and nourish and support their wives faithfully.

And how the bride agreed and said to the groom: *This is my beloved, this is my friend.* Be a husband to me and I will be your wife from this day and forever. And I will work for you and honor you and nourish you and support you in the ways of Jewish women.

And the groom agreed and said to her: Let us make a covenant, as it is written: *And I will make with you an everlasting covenant. Enlarge the place of your tent* and let us live together, beloved friends, and let us build a loyal house among the people of Israel.

And the bride agreed and said to him: Let us make a covenant to make our lives holy, with Torah, love, and good deeds. *For the mountains may move and the hills be shaken, but my trust will not leave you nor my covenant of peace fade.*

The groom _____ and the bride _____ said: All this we take upon ourselves to fulfill, with a full understanding and willingness of spirit, to the best of our abilities. *And may the grace of God be upon us and establish the work of our hands.*

Acquisition has been made from the groom to the bride and from the bride to the groom. All is valid and confirmed.

By Gilah Langner and David Drelich

Brit Kiddushin

At this time, the ___ day of _____ 57 _____ corresponding to the ___ day of ___ 20___ , we, _____ and _____ celebrate in public our choice of each other as husband and wife. We promise to love, respect and support each other as man and woman. We hope to sustain each other in a life of peace and fulfillment. We therefore pledge:

To share our lives together in joy and hardship, the everyday and the special moments; To contribute to each other's personal and emotional growth; To open ourselves to each other in trust; To be partners in decision-making, family roles, and in child-rearing, should we be so blessed; To consider each other's feelings and to settle our differences through self-examination, dialogue and compromise.

We thereby hope to become one in body and one in spirit while yet becoming more fully individual selves. And we thereby declare our intention to become a true family among the families of Israel: to have a reverence for the sacred; to sanctify our lives in Torah; to maintain consciousness of the mysteries of life; to live with reverence and compassion for all people; and to open our home to those in need.

By Rabbi Edward Feld

Ketubah of Blessing

"God sits in heaven and makes matches below." Yiddish proverb

On the ____th day of ___ (month), 20____ , the ___ th day of ___ (Hebrew month), 57 ____ , one year to the day after they declared their intention to marry in *tanayim* witnessed by loving friends, in the city of _____. _____ (groom's name), son of _____ and _____ Said to _____ (bride's name), daughter of _____ and _____ Behold you are holy to me according to the laws of Moses and Israel. I have loved you with constancy, therefore I have drawn you to me with loving kindness. (Jeremiah 31:3)

And _____ (bride's name) accepted this commitment freely, replying

This is my resting place forever. Here will I dwell, for I have desired it. (Psalms 132:14)

This couple entered into a covenant of marriage, declaring: I will cherish you and respect you and support you with faithfulness and compassion and honesty.

Let our home be a sanctuary, a place of healing and growth. Let us join together to mark the changing seasons and celebrate the traditions of our people. Let our companionship across the years be a blessing to each other and a blessing that embraces the communities in which we work and live.

Should either of us choose to end the marriage that we sanctify today

_____ and _____ agree to give each other an honorable divorce. We will convene and abide by the decision of a *bet hesed,* outlined in the separate document which we have signed, and so may no marriage among the children of Israel be bound by chains.

_____ and _____ pledge that one will protect the other from indignity at the time of death, offering tender presence with the beloved until they are separated by the grave.

All this is valid and binding.

By Debra Cash and David Fillingham[17]

The *Huppah*

The bridal canopy is a multifaceted symbol: it is a home, a garment, a bedcovering, and a reminder of the tents of nomadic ancestors. The fact that the *huppah* is open on all sides recalls in particular the tent of the biblical Abraham, a paragon of hospitality, who had doors on all four sides of his dwelling so that visitors would always know they were welcome.

In Talmudic times the groom's father set up a royal purple tent in the courtyard of his home where the marriage would be finalized by consummation. Over time, *nissuin* became a symbolic act, which the groom accomplished by covering the bride with a garment—a veil or his *tallis*—and the word *huppah* became identified with the act of "covering" or "taking" the bride.[18]

Long after tents vanished from the Jewish landscape, wedding ceremonies were held out of doors in the hope that the marriage would be blessed by as many children as "the stars of the heavens." Some kind of covering was employed to create a more modest and sanctified space, separated from the "marketplace." During the sixteenth century, probably in Poland, a portable canopy held aloft by four poles came into vogue, and over time the word *huppah* became identified more with this canopy than with its legal function of *nissuin.*

The Midrashists wrote that God created ten splendid *huppot* for the marriage of Adam and Eve. And the tabernacle built by the Israelites in the desert is also described as a bridal canopy.[19] In some European communities, richly embroidered Torah ark coverings (*parochet*) were used for weddings, but a more common custom was to marry under a *tallis,* which was frequently a gift from the bride or her family to the groom. The *tzitzit* (ritual fringes) on the prayer shawl hanging above the couple's heads were regarded as talismans against evil spirits. According to Gematria, a numerical system in which every Hebrew letter has a numerical value, the thirty-two bunches of *tzitzit* mystically correspond to the total achieved by the Hebrew word for heart, which is *lev.*

The *huppah* is understood as a sign of God's presence at the wedding and in the home being established under the canopy. *Huppah* means "that which covers or floats above." It is said that the space beneath the canopy is spiritually charged because the divine Name floats above it.

The Canopy. The *huppah* should be a temporary, handmade structure. Trees do not count, nor are *huppot* made entirely of flowers strictly kosher. Despite the fact that the canopy has a legal function, there are no *halakhic* requirements about its dimensions, shape, or decoration. Its appearance is entirely a matter of taste, another opportunity for personal expression and *hiddur mitzvah*—the beautification of piety.

Many synagogues own *huppot* they make available to marrying couples. Some of these are quite beautiful, embroidered or woven with quotations from the seven wedding blessings and decorated with familiar images—kiddush cups, doves, and scenes of Jerusalem. Synagogue *huppot* tend to be stationary structures that are set up on the *bimah* in advance of the ceremony.

Recently the use of a prayer shawl as a canopy has made a big comeback. Marrying under *tzitzit,* which are reminders of the *mitzvot,* is seen as an affirmation of the couple's commitment to a shared Jewish life. Obviously, in order to function as a *huppah,* a *tallis* needs to be a full-sized garment, one that covers two-thirds of the body. Using a grandparent's *tallis* can be very moving; if you have such a family heirloom you can use, make sure to share the story with guests.

If you will be using a stationary or floral huppah, another way to incorporate a *tallis* into the ceremony is to drape a prayer shawl over the heads of the couple under the canopy. This may be done just before the seven wedding blessings.

For people with the time and inclination, making a *huppah* can be a very satisfying project. Special talents are not necessary to create something of meaning. You can simply buy a special piece of fabric in colors and a pattern you like (three feet by five feet is a good size) and hem it. A *huppah* can be batiked, silk-screened, woven, appliquéd, or embroidered. Many needlecraft and embroidery books feature patterns that can be traced or ironed onto the fabric. (Judaica shops generally carry tablecloth patterns that can be adapted for use on a *huppah.*) The American friendship quilt has inspired some women to create individual squares that are then sewn together for the canopy.

For those who don't sew, words can be written in calligraphy or patterns hand-painted on fabric. Colorful pieces of felt can be cut and pasted in any shape or pattern. Or the *huppah* can be created at a prewedding party at which guests inscribe blessings onto a plain piece of canvas or linen with a rainbow of watercolor pens. One couple used this occasion to teach their friends some of the songs that were to be sung at the wedding. Another couple invited their nieces and nephews to decorate a *huppah* with handprints in colorful fabric paints.

The seven marriage blessings have inspired many *huppah* designs. Among the best known of these images is the "rejoicing voices": "Kol sasson v'kol simcha, kol kallah v'kol hatan" ("The voice of joy and the voice of gladness, the voice of the bride and the voice of the bridegroom"). Other traditional subjects suggested by the *sheva b'rachot* include the two cups of wine, Eden, and the streets of Jerusalem. The stars and the moon are often pictured on *huppot* as portents of children to come.[20] But there is no rule that the *huppah* must be covered with publicly recognizable images and symbols. One bride and groom, who over many years had collected frog and elephant memorabilia, incorporated their "mascots" in a scene of Jerusalem.

For Jews-by-choice, the *huppah* can be a wonderful place to incorporate designs, materials, and symbols from your family and culture of origin. A Chinese silk, Scottish tartan, or family heirloom lace canopy are more than beautiful conversation pieces; they eloquently acknowledge and honor your ethnic or cultural heritage and family.

When planning a *huppah* cover, make sure to provide some means of hanging it securely from four poles. Eyelets, curtain rings, or clasps should be fastened to the canopy so there is no danger of its slipping during the ceremony. *Tallesim* are easily hung from the eyelets for the fringes.

The poles should be long enough to stand on the ground supported rather than held by the *huppah* bearers during the ceremony. Wooden dowels, available at most lumberyards, can easily be cut to length, and bamboo is both lightweight and pretty. Wood can be carved and/or painted; ribbons, colored masking tape, crepe paper, flowers, and greenery can be used for decoration.

According to one custom, parents would plant a cypress tree on the birth of a son and a cedar on the birth of a daughter. At the time of the children's marriage, branches from each would be cut and carved for poles. Today some couples spend a day in the woods looking for appropriate branches. And one couple fastened their *huppah* to brightly colored helium balloons!

The Huppah in the Ceremony. Stationary *huppot* are usually erected before the ceremony. If, however, the canopy is to be held by four honored guests, it can become part of the processional, with the pole bearers displaying the *huppah* as they walk down the aisle.

It is a special honor to be asked to hold a *huppah* pole. The four faces surrounding the couple represent the community that will help them establish a home.* In Orthodox communities it is still customary for all the guests—except the elderly and the ill—to remain standing throughout the ceremony to acknowledge the sanctity of the proceedings. However, since it is now customary for the entire company to sit, the *huppah* bearers act as representatives of the community in this regard as well.

Although most *huppot* are raised on the *bimah,* or platform, at one end of a synagogue or function room, some couples gather their guests around them in a circle or semicircle. In this way their new "home" is surrounded by the support and love of a community. This "*huppah*-in-the-round" arrangement also enables more guests to see the faces of the bride and groom.

There are many opinions and customs regarding who should and who should not stand under the *huppah* with the couple. Some believe that in order to ensure the validity of *nissuin,* only the bride and groom (not even the rabbi) should be covered by the canopy. Others feel that many family members and friends should stand with the couple to establish the tradition of *hachnasat orchim*—hospitality—in their home. Guests who participate in the ceremony—by reading a poem or chanting one of the wedding blessings—are often invited under the *huppah* when they address the couple.

The space beneath the *huppah* is sometimes described as a spiritually charged place, a place made sacred by the presence of love, community, and God. Thus, after the bride and groom leave it, some rabbis and cantors will invite guests—especially couples—to come "inside" for a blessing or a few moments of prayer.

A Family Heirloom. People who have spent time creating a *huppah* often display or use it again after the wedding. *Huppot* commonly appear as wall hangings in couples' bedrooms. Some suspend the canopy over

* Since this is not a strictly religious duty, some rabbis suggest it as an appropriate way for non-Jewish friends to participate in the ceremony.

their beds, recalling the original use of the *huppah* as a bridal chamber. Similarly, a *huppah* can be quilted and used as a bedcovering.

Homemade *huppot* are sometimes lent to special friends and family members for use in other weddings, and a few have been donated to synagogues for community use. But, generally, couples hold on to their *huppot* with hopes of seeing their children married under it. Some raise their bridal canopy again over a son's *bris* and/or a daughter's naming ceremony.*

The Processional

In the *shtetl* it was not uncommon for everyone who could walk to turn out to accompany the bride and groom to the synagogue. Israeli kibbutzniks have been ferried to their canopies on tractors, accompanied by virtually every man, woman, and child in the community. In America it is customary for rows of identically dressed young men and women to precede the bride's climactic entrance. These and other customs grew from the ancient practice of treating brides and grooms like royalty, deserving of a regal entourage. In Jewish tradition it is both an honor and an obligation to serve the wedding king and queen. Attending the bride was considered so important by the rabbis that Rabbi Judah bar Il'ai is said to have instructed his students to put aside their studies to accompany a poor bride to her canopy.[21]

In American practice, fathers escort their daughters down the aisle to "give" them in marriage. The Jewish custom places far more emphasis on the role of both parents in leading their children—sons as well as daughters—to marriage. A traditional Jewish processional is simplicity itself: the groom is brought to the canopy by his parents, the bride is brought by her parents, and the ceremony begins. In a common variation on this theme the two fathers escort the groom, and the two mothers

* See *The New Jewish Baby Book* by Anita Diamant (Jewish Lights Publishing).

walk with the bride. Either arrangement demonstrates that marriage is a union of families, not just individuals, and acknowledges parents' dreams and efforts for their children's happiness. As there are no *halakhic* rules on the composition and arrangement of processionals, most rabbis leave the matter up to the couple.

The roles of best man and maid/matron of honor have an ancient precedent in Judaism. Gabriel and Michael, two angels said to have attended the wedding of Adam and Eve, are considered the prototypical *shushvinim*—"friends"—of the bride and groom. Traditionally, the bride and groom have two *shushvinim* each, to act as their right and left hands. The groom's *shushvinim* may be put in charge of the rings; the bride may ask hers to hold the *ketubah* during the ceremony. The Yiddish name for these honored and important members of the wedding party, *unterfuhrers,* refers to the specific task of escorting the couple to the *huppah.* In some communities the *unterfuhrers* included two married couples, specifically, people who had been married only once. If brothers and sisters fell into this category, they would perform the honor. If not, other relatives or friends were asked.[22]

Processionals can easily be adapted to accommodate particular needs, including awkward situations created by divorce. Divorced and/or remarried parents may be uncomfortable at their children's weddings, but the processional can be organized to include and honor them and minimize the strain.

If divorced parents of the bride and/or groom have an amicable relationship, they may accompany their child down the aisle. Indeed, a child remains a living sign of a dream divorced parents once shared, a dream that certainly deserves to be remembered on this occasion.[23] If this arrangement causes any difficulty, each parent may be accompanied down the aisle by another of their children or by an escort. The bride or groom can then follow his/her parents unaccompanied. Children from previous marriages can be given roles in the processional, such as carrying the *ketubah* or the rings, or if they are old enough, acting as one of the *huppah* pole bearers.

Once the bride arrives at the *huppah*, it is customary for the groom to come out, meet her, and lead her into the *huppah*. This is a ritual enactment of the bride being taken into the groom's house. Sometimes the groom and bride will kiss their parents before entering the *huppah*. Couples who prefer to begin on a symbolically equal footing walk down the aisle together.

Here are a few options for ordering a processional:

JEWISH AMERICAN
Rabbi and/or cantor (*enter from a side entrance, without ceremony*)
Bride's grandparents
Groom's grandparents
Usher,* bridesmaid
Usher, bridesmaid
Best man
Groom's father, groom, groom's mother
Usher, bridesmaid
Usher, bridesmaid
Maid of honor
Bride's father, bride, bride's mother

SECOND MARRIAGE
Huppah bearers
Rabbi or cantor
Musicians
Bride's daughter from a previous marriage carrying flowers
Mother of groom with best man
Mother of bride with brother of bride
Father of bride with maid of honor
Groom and bride

* In Orthodox settings, male and female escorts and attendants do not walk down the aisle together, and they remain separate throughout the ceremony and celebration.

Ceremonial Cup
© by Gloria Nelson

Simcha Chairs™
© by Jeanette Kuvin Oren

INTIMATE/FAMILY

Grandparents of the bride
Grandfather of the groom with granddaughter
Groom's sister and brother
Groom's father, groom, groom's mother
Bride's sister
Bride's father, bride, bride's mother

SIMPLICITY REVISITED

Groom's attendants
Groom's parents
Groom

Bride's attendants
Bride's parents
Bride

There are no laws about who stands where beneath the *huppah.* It is customary, however, for the bride to stand at the groom's right. One of the most common arrangements under the canopy looks like this:

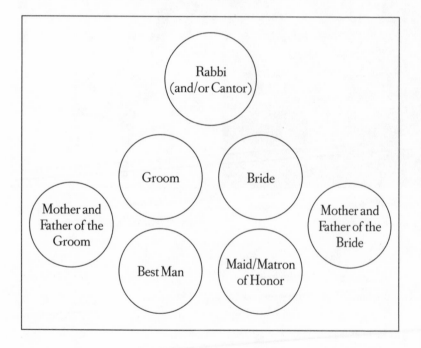

Other attendants can be seated or remain standing around the *huppah* in any order or pattern.

Planning the processional and *huppah* logistics can create conflict and anxiety, which is really the only reason to hold a wedding rehearsal. This is one area where a wedding coordinator can be of great assistance. Or assign a trusted friend or relative, who is not part of the processional, to be the "starter," who sends the wedding party down the aisle, in order and on time.

Music. The performance of music at a wedding is considered a religious obligation. In ancient times it was customary to play a flute for the bride and groom—a tradition some couples have reintroduced into the processional.

Processional music should be joyful but also purposeful and stately. (A livelier tune is usually reserved for the recessional.) It is customary for a single melody to accompany the entire processional, but if the bride is the last person to appear, one way to heighten the drama of her arrival is for the melody to change just before her entrance.

Something from the classical repertory is often played for wedding processionals, but many rabbis explicitly request that couples avoid the two most conventional selections—from Wagner's *Lohengrin* and Mendelssohn's *Midsummer Night's Dream*—pieces written by, respectively, a notorious anti-Semite and a Jew who converted to Christianity.

In the last century many American synagogues installed organs, which remain the musical standard in many communities. Although much Jewish music is not suited to the harmonic mode of the organ, simple, melodic arrangements can be quite beautiful. If you use the synagogue's organist, make an appointment to select music and musical styles, and if you have a favorite song you'd like played, find the sheet music and bring it to your meeting.

Israeli melodies, arranged for any combination of instruments and voices, make lovely processional accompaniments. Many of the most popular Hebrew songs for processionals are settings of poems from the Song of Songs, among them "Dodi li" (I Am My Beloved's), "Iti Mil'Vanon" (Come with Me from Lebanon), and "Hanava Babanot" (Beautiful One). Other favorites include "Erev Shel Shoshanim" (Evening of Roses) and "Chorshat Haekalyptus" (The Eucalyptus Grove). Other sources for processional melodies include Yiddish folk songs and Sephardic music. Cantors are wonderful resources for wedding music. To find sheet music and recordings of all sorts of wedding music, look in Jewish bookstores and in synagogue libraries. Many congregations permit nonmembers to browse and copy.[24]

There is no good substitute for live music during the processional. A soloist playing virtually any instrument sets a mood (or, in biblical parlance, "gladdens the heart") as nothing else can.

Any combination of instruments or voices can be effective accompaniment for the processional. Some common groupings are: guitar-recorder duet; string quartet; and flute, acoustic guitar, and cello. Orchestras and bands that play wedding receptions often include a flute player, who can provide the processional melody.

Another way of greeting the couple with music is for the guests to sing as the bride and groom walk to the *huppah;* Yemenite brides are sometimes preceded by a group of singing women. A trio or quartet of friends singing an Israeli love song in harmony can provide a very moving background. Or the rabbi, cantor, or *mesader kiddushin*, can, in a matter of minutes, teach all the guests a *niggun,* a wordless melody. No welcome to the *huppah* could be warmer or more personal than the voices of the people you love.

Candles. Light is a universal symbol of God's presence. The soft light of candles, which are associated with the joy of Shabbat and the holidays, can add a beautiful dimension to an evening ceremony. In some communities it is customary for those who lead the couple to the canopy to light the way with burning candles. In the past it was common for all the guests to carry candles—or torches—thus providing the light by which the ceremony was conducted. At the end of the ceremony these were tossed into the air along with the shouts of *"Mazel tov!"*

The beautiful braided candles of *havdalah* are often used for processionals, and these are now available in rainbows of color as well as the traditional blue and white. If, however, candles will be held by more than one or two members of the processional, it's probably wise to use dripless tapers and some sort of candle holders. Also, before proceeding with plans that include candles, make sure there are no problems with fire laws.

At one wedding each guest was handed a candle as she/he entered the sanctuary. The first two people in the processional acted as light bearers, row by row illuminating the candles of the people on the aisle, who in turn lit the candles of the people seated next to them, creating an ever-widening circle of light as the bride and groom walked into the room.

Some rabbis ask that the couple provide a pair of candlesticks under the *huppah,* which are meant to symbolize the beginning of a home that will be filled with the light of Shabbat and festival candles. When the bride and groom have arrived under the canopy, two attendants might light one candle each while someone reads this lesson, attributed to the Baal Shem Tov: "From every human being there rises a light that reaches straight to heaven. And when two souls that are destined for each other find one another, their streams of light flow together and a single brighter light goes forth from their united being."[25]

Circling. While there is a biblical source for the custom "A woman shall go around a man" (Jeremiah 31:22), the bride's circling the groom before entering the *huppah* is not part of the wedding liturgy. It is, however, a very old custom, which varies in practice; some circle three times, some seven times. Some brides are led around the groom by both mothers, and sometimes the entire processional circles him.

There are many explanations for the practice. Circling is a magical means of protection. By walking around the groom the bride creates an invisible wall to protect him from evil spirits, from the glances of other women, and from the temptations of the world. The bride's circle may also be seen as a way of binding the groom to her. Her circuits symbolically create a new family circle, demonstrating that her primary allegiance has shifted from her parents to her husband and that her husband is now bound to her more intimately than to his parents.[26]

Whether one performs three or seven circuits is a matter of family and community custom. Some base a preference for three on the repetition in the Bible: "And I will betroth you to me forever. I will betroth you to me in righteousness, and in justice, and in loving-kindness, and in compassion; and I will betroth you to me in faithfulness" (Hosea 2:19). Also, a husband must fulfill three obligations to his wife: provide food and clothing and observe conjugal relations.

Jewish mystics preferred the number seven. Sevens abound in the Bible and throughout Jewish life. The world was created in seven days, and marriage is a seven-days-a-week act of creation. With marriage, seven of the bride's relatives are forbidden to the groom.[27] There are seven wedding blessings. And circling is thought of as the way the bride enters the groom's *s'ferot*—the mystical spheres of his soul that correspond to the seven lower attributes of God.

Many liberal Jews abandoned the custom because of its magical connotations and because of the apparent subservience in the bride's circuits around her "master." Recently, however, many couples have reclaimed this custom with both new interpretations and new ritual forms. Some women have reintroduced the bride's circling, seeing it not as a token of subservience but as a powerful act of definition: she creates the space the couple will share.

Many couples prefer to mutualize this gesture. At some weddings the bride circles the groom clockwise (three or seven times), and then the groom repeats the gesture counterclockwise around the bride, or bride and groom hold hands and walk in a circle, ring-around-the-rosie style. Either way, the double circling physically demonstrates independent and complementary orbits. This kind of circling has been accompanied by strains of music or with the words of a poem or prayer found or written for the occasion. This is another place that *Shir haShirim*, the Song of Songs, is especially appropriate.

The Recessional. After the glass is broken the bride and groom leave the *huppah* to the sounds of joyous, up-tempo music. One of the most popular selections for this is the Israeli song "Od Yishama" (Again Will Be Heard). Other common songs are "Siman Tov u'Mazel Tov" (A Good Sign and Good Luck) and "Yasis Alayich" (May God Rejoice) or any upbeat song.[28]

The notion of a formal recessional developed at least in part to facilitate the receiving line. After the bride and groom made their exit, the parents of the couple walked back up the aisle, followed by the rabbi, grandparents, and attendants. Generally, members of the processional leave in the reverse order of their arrival.

If the couple is going to *yichud*, the customary ten to fifteen minutes of seclusion, there is no receiving line and therefore less need for a recessional. Once the bride and groom leave, the parents of the couple embrace and guests surround them with congratulations. If the celebration is to be held at the same location, hors d'oeuvres and champagne are served immediately. At high-spirited weddings the music that greets the breaking of the glass is the signal for dancing to begin. In some cases guests will dance, accompanying the bride and groom to *yichud*.

The Receiving-Line Dilemma. *Yichud* means never having to stand on a receiving line—a welcome excuse for people who dread the drawn-out, repetitive ritual of meeting and greeting that is standard practice at American weddings.

Receiving lines do, of course, fulfill important functions. For one thing, they give parents a chance to *kvell*—to bask in their children's happiness. Also, a formal line means the couple has the opportunity to at least say hello to all their guests, something that might not otherwise happen. It means everyone gets the chance to meet all the principals and allows people to match names and faces. "So *you're* Cousin Susan!" "So *you're* the friend who flew in from Israel!" "So you're Myra's mother!"

But receiving lines are also something of an ordeal, especially at a wedding of any size. For the guests the waiting is always a little awkward, and then there's never enough time to say more than a quick "Mazel tov."

After a while the receivers are bound to get tired (not to mention hungry), and their greetings and smiles begin to feel wooden.

When *yichud* is observed, many couples simply forgo the receiving line and allow guests to seek them out for a private moment during the celebration. Of course, the couple's families can still create a receiving line to accept congratulations and *kvell.* (If this is your plan, and your parents will be meeting many of your friends for the first time, it's helpful to get an attendant to stand in line and help with introductions.) Some couples have come up with alternatives to the receiving line that ensure them the chance to share a word with all their guests during the *simcha.* These are described in the following chapters.

Witnesses

A marriage can be valid without a rabbi but not without witnesses. Since witnessing is considered a great responsibility, the bride and groom should select witnesses they trust and respect. Because they are so important in "making" the marriage, it has been suggested that witnesses assume a responsibility that lasts "for one hundred and twenty years"—the number of years Moses was said to live.

The Hebrew word for "witness," *ayd,* shares a common root with the word *od,* meaning "duration"; a witness gives permanence to human activities that are transitory.[29] While a room filled with people might see a wedding take place, only the designated witnesses have the power to validate the subtle transaction at the core of the ceremony.* The rabbis understood that family members might have more of an emotional, social,

---

* Some authorities claim that the two people who witness the *ketubah* should not be the same ones who witness the wedding. This opinion provides another opportunity to involve and honor a few more special friends in the ceremony. However, there is disagreement on this point, and in many cases the same people witness both *ketubah* and ceremony.

or even economic stake in what transpired under the *huppah,* which is why *unrelated* observers are specified.

Because they play such a vital role, there have always been strict and specific laws about who is a kosher witness. According to halakhah, witnesses must be observant Jewish men over the age of thirteen who are unrelated to each other or to the bride or groom. If these conditions are not met, the marriage is legally suspect, which is why it became customary for the officiating cantor and rabbi to serve as witnesses.

Jewish law's "exemption" of women from participation in communal worship and public events is usually attributed to the Talmud's respect for their special duties in the home. While many Jews no longer recognize the validity of this ruling, and it is common for women to act as witnesses at liberal Jewish weddings, those who wish to fulfill the letter of the law but also want to affirm the presence and participation of women sometimes name two Jewish men and two Jewish women as their witnesses.

Criteria for what constitutes an observant Jew obviously invite disagreement. In some circles observance is equated with the title *shomer shabbos,* someone who obeys the commandments regarding Shabbat, who also obeys the laws of *kashrut,* and is mindful of the Torah's moral commandments. Of course a Jew considered "observant" by one group of people might be considered a heretic by another, but it is considered a sin to embarrass anyone with inquisitions into his or her personal habits and religious practice. According to the rabbinic adage, "One who shames his neighbor has no share in the world to come." [30]

Non-Jews are not permitted to act as witnesses because they are not bound to the religious and legal system that sanctions a Jewish marriage. Few rabbis will accept non-Jewish witnesses, although those who do not abide by other *halakhic* rules (regarding gender, for instance) may permit a non-Jew who is informed of the duties and obligations entailed by this honor.

At the *ketubah* signing or before the ceremony begins, the rabbi may introduce the witnesses and explain their responsibilities. Sometimes witnesses are questioned (gently) to make sure they are qualified and understand their role and to determine whether they are willing to stand by the couple through the challenges and difficulties of their marriage.

The witnesses are assigned a position where they can see and hear the bride and groom. The bride and groom must also be able to see the witnesses and be aware of their identity and role. In traditional ceremonies the rabbi asks that the witnesses examine the ring and testify that it is worth one *prutah,* the smallest coin used in ancient times, before the groom gives it to the bride. The witnesses must see him put the ring on her finger and hear his recitation of the marriage formula: "*Harey aht me'kudeshet li . . .*" (With this ring you are consecrated to me . . .). Although the bride is not required to say anything in response, the witnesses must see that she willingly consents to the marriage.

Witnesses are sometimes asked to attest to the validity of the couple's *yichud* as well. They watch the bride and groom enter a room they have determined to be empty, stand guard over the couple's privacy, and as wife and husband emerge.

A Jewish Checklist

Weddings breed lists at an alarming rate, but it's a good idea to have one special list for ceremonial items. On the day of the wedding it should be entrusted to a reliable person (but *not* the bride or groom) who will make sure everything is ready and in place:

- Table(s) and tablecloths (for *ketubah* signing, and under the *huppah*)
- *Ketubah* and pen (with correct color of ink!)
- *Huppah* and poles
- *Kiddush* cups and wine
- Glass for breaking (in a napkin or pouch)
- Rings
- Candles and matches
- Wedding booklets
- *Kippot* (yarmulkes) for guests
- Signs that direct guests to groom's table and bride's room

PLANNING
THE PARTY

Making It a Simcha. The meal that follows a Jewish wedding is called a *s'eudah mitzvah,* a meal to accompany the fulfillment of a religious commandment.* According to tradition, any communal meal can be consecrated if it includes some religious content, some "words of Torah." According to *Pirke Avot* (Words of the Fathers), ". . . if three have eaten at a table and have spoken words of Torah, it is as if they have eaten from the table of God." At a wedding, everything that increases happiness praises God: words of Torah, blessings, songs, dances, toasts, reminiscences, and jokes that make the bride and groom laugh.

"Reception" is not the right word for what happens after the *huppah; simcha* is more accurate. *Simcha* means "joy" as well as the "celebration of a joyous event," and the purpose of Jewish wedding parties is to increase the happiness of the bride and groom. The Talmud says that someone who enjoys a wedding feast but does nothing to rejoice the hearts of the bride and groom has transgressed against the "five voices": the voice of joy, the voice of gladness, the voice of the bridegroom, the voice of the bride, and the voice that praises God. This section offers ideas and strategies for fulfilling the holiest, happiest goal of the wedding celebration—increasing the *simcha* of bride and groom.

---

* In addition to weddings, *s'eudot mitzvah* follow major life-cycle events, including circumcision, bar or bat mitzvah, the completion of a course of Jewish study, conversion to Judaism, and funerals.

Food and Drink

Kashrut. Planning the menu for a *s'eudah mitzvah* requires giving some thought to *kashrut*—the system of laws that govern what and how Jews eat. By following *kashrut* you avoid discomfort—and hunger—for observant relatives and friends. Indeed, your rabbi may not be able to enjoy (or even feel able to attend) your *simcha* if the food is nonkosher. Providing a meal that conforms to the fundamentals of *kashrut* announces your intention to honor Jewish law, even if you don't plan to establish a kosher kitchen in your home.

Kashrut is best understood not as an ancient means of preserving human health but as a way of sanctifying a basic need. "Israel is commanded to hallow the act of eating and through this making holy, become holy."[31] It is based on specific proscriptions in the Bible, such as those against eating birds of prey and bottom-feeding fish. The separation of dairy and meat products is an elaboration on the Torah's command not to "boil a kid in its mother's milk."

In a nutshell, *kashrut* permits the following foods to be eaten: all vegetables and fruits, fish with fins and scales (no shellfish), domestic fowl, and animals that both chew their cud and have split hooves. For meat to be kosher, however, the animal must be killed according to specific ritual laws by someone who recites a blessing, and then soaked and salted to remove any trace of blood. Finally, meat and milk products are not eaten at the same meal and must be kept separate. To fully observe this injunction, *milchig* (dairy) and *fleishig* (meat) foods are not cooked in the same pots or served on the same dishes. The customary waiting period between consumption of meat and milk varies from one to six hours.[32]

Synagogues usually require that food be prepared and served in accordance with the dietary laws. Many congregations provide couples with a guidebook for use in their kitchens, and some allow only selected kosher caterers to work in their kitchens. Your rabbi should be able to direct you to local kosher caterers, and the Yellow Pages of most large towns and cities often have a special listing of kosher services under "Catering." Check the local Jewish newspaper too. "Kosher style" denotes Jewish-identified foods such as lox and knishes, but it is generally a signal that *kashrut* is not observed.

Given the recent trend toward leaner diets and the fact that most families now include some vegetarians, a dairy meal that features fish (which is *pareve*—neither milk nor meat) is the simplest solution to a whole range of dietary requirements. In the past, caterers did their best to dissuade people from this kind of meal, in large part because meat entrées are much more profitable. But since fish is a fashionable main course, caterers are more than willing and able to provide a full-course *milchig* meal.

Coping with Caterers. A wise rabbi once conferred the title "Levites" upon all caterers.[33] While members of this tribe were not priests (Kohanim) but assistants to priests, they performed indispensable and holy duties in the Temple. But when Levites begin to act like Kohanim—if your caterer obscures the simple truth that it is her function to make things easy for you and not vice versa—you may be headed for trouble.

The food at a wedding celebration should add to the pleasure of the bride and groom. If you hate sushi canapés, don't order them even if the caterer insists they're a specialty and your guests will be expecting them. Ask questions. Negotiate. Shop around. Even if your choices are limited because you're looking for a kosher caterer in a small city, the same criteria apply to all Levites, everywhere.

The best way to find a good caterer is by word of mouth. Ask everyone you know—from the rabbi to colleagues at work—for suggestions. If you're browsing through the Yellow Pages, pay attention to the smaller ads and single-line entries with interesting names. There are increasing numbers of "boutique" kosher caterers, who take great pride in serving beautiful, gourmet food that conforms to the dietary laws. Keep your eyes open for specialty shops that sell homemade salads, soups, breads, and desserts; many of these retail businesses also run catering services.

Remember, too, that your favorite restaurant may serve special meals in their dining room, in your rented hall, or in a private home. Vegetarian restaurants can be a good source for *milchig* meals.

Before calling a caterer be ready with the following information: the date and time of your wedding, number of guests, location, and cooking facilities. (You can't expect anyone to provide a full-course dinner for three hundred in a closet-sized kitchen.) And be prepared to give the caterer some idea of your budget. (It's not a great idea to look for bargains, however; if the price is too good to be true, the food isn't going to be.) With this information, the caterer should be able to determine whether he's able to and interested in doing your wedding.

If the person on the other end of the line is curt, impatient, or in any way unpleasant, call another caterer. Graciousness is an important part of serving a meal, and your initial contact is a pretty good indicator of what you can expect from further dealings. You're going to be working closely with this person, so if you feel any discomfort, look for someone else. When you find an amiable, recommended caterer who is willing and able to take on your wedding, make an appointment to meet. Some caterers will charge a fee for an initial consultation and tasting.

Before your meeting, make notes about what you would and would not like to have served. Some caterers show sample menus and even photographs of their work, but it is most important to get a list of recent clients as references. Any reputable caterer will be happy to provide you with some. (When you check references, make sure to ask about the quantity as well as the quality of the food.) In some cases you might even arrange to discreetly watch a caterer in action—but don't expect free samples.

Caterers charge on a per-person basis for either sit-down or buffet meals. A last-minute guest or two extra rarely presents a problem, but if twenty "extras" arrive at the buffet table, you risk not having enough food, and the caterer will legitimately charge for them. Don't forget to count the musicians and photographer.

Caterers usually ask for a deposit of 30 to 50 percent of their estimate, with the balance due on the day of the wedding. Many states have a meal tax that is added to the bill. No matter whom you choose as a caterer, it is essential to have a written contract that spells out your agreement. This doesn't have to be an elaborate document; it can be a simple letter or memo that itemizes the particulars, including date, menu, and an estimate of the price.

The caterer's price may include any and all of the following: rental of linen, china, silverware; liquor, the wedding cake, waiters and bartenders, and, in some cases, even musicians. If the caterer provides a full bar, for example, you'll be paying for the time he spends ordering the liquor as well as for the beverages, plus some markup.

Wedding consultants, or "accommodators," are contractors who can be hired to do all the planning. They will rent the hall, tables, chairs, linens, dishes, and glassware; find and hire the caterer, band, and cleanup crew; even tend to the printing of the invitations and newspaper announcements. Again, the best way to find an accommodator is by word of mouth.

If your wedding is informal and/or you want to minimize expenses, a caterer can be hired as an "expediter" rather than the sole provisioner. Professional supervision over a carefully orchestrated potluck meal can result in an elegant yet "haimish" or homey repast.

Wedding Cakes.

Weddings mean cakes. For some people it's not a *real* wedding without a four-foot-tall, three-tiered white cake with bride and groom statuettes on the top. For others it's not a wedding without a piece of *laykach*—sponge cake—with a glass of Manischewitz sweet blackberry wine to wash it down.

Caterers who do a lot of weddings can provide a cake to your specifications. But there are also specialty bakers who create real works of art out of sugar and flour. These are, of course, very expensive and priced by the slice. Be sure to taste before you buy.

Le'chaim. Jews have long considered drink a legitimate tool for creating *simcha*. The open bar has recently become a common feature at Jewish weddings, finally disproving (for better or worse) the truism "Jews don't drink." But the bar, like the menu, can reflect your tastes and preferences. Champagne, wine, and beer in abundance can certainly suffice. And there should always be plenty of nonalcoholic beverages as well.

As far as *kashrut*'s application to potables is concerned, the Torah prohibits Jews from drinking any wine that has been used in connection with idolatry. The Talmud later extended this prohibition to all wines produced by non-Jews, although the restriction never applied to wine made from fruit other than grapes or to grain liquors. Many non-Orthodox synagogues allow wine that is not designated "kosher." Some couples make a point of serving Israeli wine, both to support Israel and as a sign of Jewish identification.

Laughter, Music, and Dance

Reinventing the Badchan. Spontaneous observance of the ancient injunction to "rejoice the bride and groom" usually requires some careful groundwork. This need not (and should not) involve much time or effort from bride or groom on the day of the wedding—a little delegating of responsibility and some explicit hinting beforehand should suffice.

One couple added a note on the map to their synagogue that said: "Jewish tradition treats the bride and groom as king and queen. The main purpose of the wedding party is to entertain the couple. In this spirit we hope you'll come prepared with a story, a poem, a joke to tell, a song to sing—maybe even a magic trick—along with your best dancing shoes and a happy heart." The results of this hint included everything from poems to shaggy-dog stories, from an eight-year-old's violin debut to song parodies and even a magic trick!

These entertainments were presented during the wedding feast, introduced by a master of ceremonies, a close friend who had long harbored a secret ambition to be a stand-up comedian. His monologue included sight gags and toasts, the story of how the bride and groom met, and amusing introductions for every "act." He announced the start of the dancing and informed the company when dessert was served. Most important, he set a joyful example.

In other words, he acted as a modern-day *badchan*, literally, "joker." Also called *leytzan*, clown, or *marshalik*, marshal, the *badchan* was an indispensable part of Eastern European weddings for nearly seven centuries. The term *badchan* comes from a word that means "to cheer up" or "to make laugh." He was a paid professional, a combination jester, preacher, singer, rhymester, and toastmaster. He could be crude and earthy, and announced the size of cash gifts. But he was also supposed to be a learned man whose witticisms were based in biblical verses and passages of Talmud. He told anecdotes about the guests, he posed riddles, he dispensed compliments; in other words, he could really make or break a *simcha*.[34]

An accomplished *badchan* would elicit tears as well as laughter. One of his most important duties was presiding at the *bedeken*, at which he was expected to make a sentimental speech to the bride about the cruel passage of time. But the *badchan*'s primary function was to make people laugh. Like all good comedians, he made light of current tensions. The *badchan* has been credited with keeping Jewish humor alive even during some of Eastern European Jewry's darkest hours. Indeed, the flowering of Yiddish theater and literature in the nineteenth and early twentieth centuries probably owes a great deal to the persistence of *badchanut*—the art of the *badchan*.

It is not difficult to reinvent the *badchan* for modern purposes. All that is needed is a willing friend or member of the family, someone who knows how to tell a joke, who is willing to share the microphone, who is not afraid to make a fool of him- or herself. Once the bride and groom entrust someone with the job, the *badchan* should be allowed free reign and should be given background information on both families, the more personal, the better.

The *badchan* may also have more serious emcee responsibilities, such as making the first toast, announcing dinner, reading messages from absent friends or family members, introducing the band, and leading the company in the blessings after the meal. As with *badchanut* of old, sentiment plays an indispensable role. The master of ceremonies can give people permission to put their feelings into words, with toasts offered as blessings. She/he may invite the learned guests to give a *vort* or *d'var Torah*—some thoughts about the week's Torah portion. Guests may compose original poems and songs to honor the bride and groom; others might want to read a favorite quotation or poem.

The *badchan*'s main task is to orchestrate the entertainment, to which end she/he may wish to line up some speakers and performers or even instigate some *mishegas* (foolishness) in advance of the wedding.

One *badchan* began by "crowning" the couple with foil-covered crowns and scepters and leading them to a pair of elaborately decorated "thrones," which were wheeled in by a few costumed co-conspirators, who then proceeded to juggle—very badly and very funnily.

Song parodies (set to any popular tune) about the bride and groom are common, and lyrics can even be printed and distributed to all the guests for a comic serenade.

Other forms of modern *badchanut* have included card tricks, acrobatics, and vaudeville routines. At one wedding a dramatization of the couple's first date was performed by two of the youngest children present. In preparation for another wedding, some enterprising friends got the bride and groom to pose for pictures, which they then developed into a kind of "This Is Your Life" slide show. One *badchan,* a gifted improviser, distributed cards and asked guests to return them with questions they'd always wanted to ask about Jewish weddings—and answered them all with outrageous lies.

Historically, Jewish wedding celebrations have reflected the state of the arts of the culture and time. During the Italian Renaissance, guests composed sonnets and performed elaborate pageants and plays as grand and as elegant as anything the secular culture had to offer. At Yemenite weddings, professional singers and dancers are sometimes hired to perform. Today an original videotape could be part of the *simcha*.

Music. There is a Hasidic saying, "When two who cannot sing raise their voices together, a miracle happens." Anything from sentimental ballads to silly parodies to folk tunes to camp songs can turn a group of strangers into a community. Song sheets and a willing song leader can help unite the guests into an unforgettable serenade for the bride and groom. (Guitars are helpful in this but not crucial.)

There is no rule against hiring a string quartet to provide stately classical music while your guests mingle and eat. However, since dancing is a traditional and treasured feature of Jewish weddings (see below), dance bands are generally preferred.

Regular wedding bands tend to have a broad, standard repertoire ranging from rock 'n' roll hits (1950s to the present), big band tunes, and a "Jewish medley" that is bound to include "Siman Tov U Mazel Tov," "Hava Nagila," and possibly songs from *Fiddler on the Roof.* Whomever you hire, make sure the leader understands what you do and don't expect of him. If you don't want to hear "Sunrise, Sunset," make that clear. If a *badchan* will be running the show, inform the bandleader that you expect him to take his cues from your master of ceremonies. Even if there's no *badchan,* appoint an ambassador to the bandleader to let your wishes be known. And, of course, never hire a band without a hearing; if a live audition is impossible, at least get hold of a tape.

Klezmer music is the classic music of Jewish weddings. *Klezmer,* a term that refers to both the music and the musicians, was once so traditional at Eastern European weddings that the phrase "like a wedding without *klezmorim*" described any lifeless, colorless event.[35] The music is a mishmash of influences: military marches, melodies by the great masters, folk songs, and dance tunes. When klezmer came to America, new instruments were added and jazz licks crept in.

In the 1950s and sixties, most of the Jewish community dismissed the music as embarrassing, unsophisticated, and overly sentimental. But in the 1980s, young musicians reclaimed the old forms; reinvigorated them with new orchestrations, blues, and rock licks; and reintroduced them to new audiences. The revival in klezmer music and the advent of the new Jewish wedding are part of the same longing for a meaning-filled connection to the past.

Once limited to big cities with large Jewish populations, klezmer groups of all shapes and sizes—from small combos to big bands—may be found throughout North America. To find the best klezmorim in your community, ask for recommendations from your rabbi and/or cantor, friends, your caterer, photographer, and florist. Check the local Jewish newspaper where bands advertise and peruse the Internet for interesting klezmer sites.

If you can't find a klezmer band or simply prefer more of a musical mix at your simcha, you can still add some of the spirit of this "roots music." Wedding bands tend to be accommodating, and if you give the bandleader some sheet music, he may be willing to play a few numbers. A simpler alternative is to play klezmer discs while the band is on break. Of course, a disc jockey or an evening of taped music is an inexpensive alternative to hiring a live band and allows you even more flexibility in selecting the music for your simcha.[36]

Dancing. The Talmud asks, "How should one dance before the bride?" Judah bar Ilai answered by dancing with a myrtle twig. Rabbi Aha danced with the bride on his shoulders. Even as a very old man, Samuel bar Rav Isaac would perform his wedding specialty—juggling three myrtle twigs while he danced and sang. At his funeral a heavenly flame burned above his coffin as God's token of appreciation for those pious performances.[37]

Jewish wedding dances are probably as old as Jewish weddings. In the Song of Songs there is mention of a "dance of two companies." Even after the rabbis grew suspicious of celebrations that threw men and women into each other's arms, dancing remained a cherished feature of wedding celebrations. While ballroom music and dancing are still the standard at American weddings, the klezmer revival has made inroads on the dance floor too.

Dancing to klezmer and Israeli folk music tends to involve groups of people rather than couples. The steps can be as simple as walking or skipping in time to the music, so all that's required are some infectious tunes and a core of enthusiasts. The *badchan* or someone else can act as "dance master," announcing: "This *freilach* [happy song] is for men only" or "All couples who have been married for less than five years up next; women line up on this side, the men on that side, clapping hands, walk to the middle of the room," and so on. This kind of dancing sweeps nearly everyone onto the dance floor—even people who insist they can't dance.

Israeli dancing ranges from simple circle dances to elaborate duets. Friends who are accomplished folk dancers might perform some of the more complex steps—especially those set to lyrics from *Shir haShirim* (Song of Songs)—and teach a few simple dances.

In Eastern European tradition, one of the first dances is usually some version of the *Mitzvah Tanz,* the dance of the commandment. Since dancing with the bride is a *mitzvah,* and since every *mitzvah* deserves individual celebration, it became customary for everyone to have a turn with the bride. The fathers usually went first, then the bridegroom, and scholars and important members of the community next. This *mitzvah* was so important that brides would invite beggars to dance with them as an act of *tsedakah* (charity).

Modern versions of the *Mitzvah Tanz* include women as well as men, all of whom try to dance for at least a moment with both the bride and groom. Sometimes this begins with the groom asking his mother to dance, and then the bride's mother. Meanwhile the bride dances with her father, and then her husband's father. Next, all the women circle the bride, and all the men circle the groom, and each dancer enters the middle to take a quick turn with the wedding queen or king.

Perhaps the best known of all Jewish wedding-dance customs is the moment at which the bride and groom are raised on the shoulders of their guests—usually in chairs. This happens at the height of the festivities, or whenever the melody and mood is right. Sometimes the couple will be whirled around each other, holding the ends of a handkerchief; sometimes the couple is paraded around the room in a processional. One theory for the origin of this custom is that during the days when bride and groom were separated by a *mechitzah*—a physical barrier between the sexes—the added height let them catch a glimpse of each other. But the custom probably has as much to do with the privileges of royalty, who have been carried in chairs and on litters from earliest times.

There are dozens of *tanzen*, dances associated with weddings. The following are some of the simple combinations and story dances that can be announced and improvised:

- The *Machetunim Tanz* gets the newly related families out on the dance floor together.
- The *Bobbes Tanz* is reserved for grandmothers only.
- In the *Broiges Tanz* a man and woman pantomime a quarrel and reconciliation.
- In the *Huppah Tanz* friends whirl around the bride and groom holding a *tallis* or a tablecloth over their heads.
- In the *Besem Tanz* a broom is a prop used as a horse, a yoke, a musical instrument, or anything else that occurs to the dancer. In pantomime dances like this one, it's common to act out the stages of a marriage: courting, *huppah*, work, children, old age.
- The *Flash Tanz* requires some skill and rehearsal since it involves balancing a bottle on the forehead or on top of the head while moving to the music.

- There are countless kinds of *freilachs*—happy songs—and these inspire all kinds of horseplay, from tying napkins together for a session of jump rope to a full-fledged Jewish square dance, complete with allemandes. Cossack dances such as the *Kazatsky* feature strenuous deep-knee-bend kicks and often lead to contests of skill, strength, and endurance.
- The song "Keytzed M'Rakdim Lifnei Hakallah" (How Should One Dance before the Bride?) is sometimes performed in lines facing the bride and groom. Groups of women and men walk toward the couple and meet in the center of the dance floor for curtsies, bows, and other movements.
- The *Mezinke*, usually performed to the Yiddish song "Die Mezinke Oysgegeben" (The Youngest Daughter Is Given), is one of the last dances. This is a tribute to a mother who has brought her last daughter to the canopy. Today the custom is commonly extended to both father and mother to commemorate their last child's *huppah*—son or daughter. Seated on chairs in the center of the dance floor, the parents are presented with bouquets and circled by the company in a dance that celebrates the completion of their parental responsibility. A variation of this theme is the *Krenzl*, or crowning (usually with a wreath of flowers) of the mother (or mothers) who has just seen her last child wed. "Die Mezinke Oysgegeben" is anything but a sad song. One of the lyrics asks, "Isaac, you rascal, why is your bow silent? Are the musicians playing or sleeping? Have them tear the strings apart. My youngest daughter is getting married!"

Of course, not all the dancing has to be "Jewish." Any music—from big-band tunes to current pop songs—that gets people up and rejoicing is a *mitzvah*. Indeed, many Eastern European and Israeli dances are based on the local steps of neighboring communities. The hora, for example, perhaps the best known of all Jewish dances, started as a Romanian folk dance!

Photographers and Flowers

Weddings are for rejoicing, not posing. But you can never have too many pictures of your own wedding. What's a couple to do?

Most couples hire a professional photographer to ensure that they get good pictures not only of themselves, but also of the most important people in their lives, convened for their special day. Likewise, most brides and grooms want the "standard" images for their albums, and for good reason; these pictures will take their place in a gallery of family portraits. Even the corniest poses, like cutting the cake, assume historical proportions when placed next to a nearly identical shot of your parents doing precisely the same thing thirty-five years ago.

Wedding photography is big business but it's also a very personal transaction, so trust your heart while shopping for a person who will be with you during this wonderful, but stressful, event. While it is important to compare technical skills and price packages, pay attention to the photographer's promptness, courtesy, and flexibility in meeting your needs.

Generally, the best way to find a photographer is through word of mouth. Ask other couples for recommendations and look at their wedding albums. Your rabbi, cantor, caterer, and florist deal with many photographers and may have favorites. Of course, photographers also advertise in newspapers—especially in special issues devoted to weddings. Many may now be found, with galleries to showcase their services, on the Web.

Plan to interview a few photographers and ask to see their work. Before the interview, think about what kind of images you want: traditional posed portraits in black and white or color, a photojournalistic record of the event, or some of each. Ask for references. If you are dealing with a large studio that employs several people, make sure to meet and see samples of the photographer assigned to your wedding.

Photographers offer a wide range of "packages" that may include proofs, albums for parents as well as the couple, wall portraits, even a mounted photo sign-in board for the guests. Generally, negatives are not included.

Some of the formal portraits and family portraits may be shot in the weeks prior to the wedding. This eases the stress of the day and permits the couple and families to celebrate with guests rather than disappear for a long time. (The injunction against seeing the bride in her dress before the wedding is *not* a Jewish custom; indeed, the groom is supposed to see the bride and lower her veil in order to insure he is marrying the right person.)

To insure that you get the pictures you want on the day of the wedding itself, give your photographer a schedule of the events you want him or her to shoot and also a list of people you especially want photos of. (Pictures of the immediate family may be obvious, but what about your favorite but shy Aunt Ruth or your friend who flew in from Argentina for the wedding?) The more thorough your list, the better. Even if she is familiar with Jewish weddings, tell the photographer about the particulars of yours. Do you want her at the *ketubah* signing and the veiling? Do you want pictures of the wedding challah and the blessing before the meal? Do you want her to concentrate on the dancing or is it more important to get a clear shot of every table?

Videography. A video record of a wedding can include everything from selecting the gown to the ceremony under the *huppah* to the tossing of the bouquet. Though some rabbis discourage or prohibit filming during the ceremony itself, others permit it because it is generally less obtrusive than flash photography. If you decide to videotape your wedding, proceed as you would with a still photographer: get recommendations from friends and other wedding professionals. Some photography studios offer both services.

Try to view the wedding videos of friends before shopping for a videographer so you'll be able to select from among the services and "packages" offered. You may be asked how long a tape you want (ninety minutes to two hours), one camera or two. Many companies offer services such as the production of an introductory montage of childhood photographs of the bride and groom set to music.

When you go to the studio to view samples, keep an eye on focus and color quality. Make sure the sample s the work of the person who will be shooting your wedding and also find out who will be editing your video. Ask about lighting since on-camera lights are less invasive than standing lights. Finally, select someone you find both skilled and pleasant. Remember, this person is going to be part of your wedding day.

Flowers. Wedding flowers are a wonderful extravagance and a reminder of the first wedding that took place in Eden, where all the blossoms of creation bloomed together. The perfume of the flowers—like the scent of the spice box in the havdalah ceremony—is a hint of paradise. *Huppah* poles offer a wonderful opportunity for the creative use of flowers and fresh greens.

In line with the wedding's celebration of life, some couples choose centerpieces of live plants. If armloads of cut flowers adorn your celebration, it is in the best spirit of Jewish tradition to ask friends to take them to a hospital or nursing home after the festivities, to share the joy of your day.

Tsedakah. According to Jewish tradition, joyous occasions of all kinds—the birth of a baby, a bar or bat mitzvah, a wedding—are celebrated not only with singing and dancing and eating, but also with charitable donations, or *tsedakah,* a word based on the Hebrew *tsedek,* which means justice. Giving *tsedakah* is a way of spreading the joy of the occasion while acknowledging that even the greatest personal happiness is incomplete as long as the world is so badly in need of repair. A donation made to honor a wedding is also a kind of investment in a happier future for the couple—and their children.

Judaism does not view charity as an act of personal goodness but as a *mitzvah,* a holy obligation, and a privilege for the giver. The reason many

Jews make contributions in multiples of eighteen dollars is that the numerical value of eighteen is spelled out with the same Hebrew letters that mean life—*chai*. Although it is customary to give money to Jewish organizations, donations can also be made to efforts and institutions that have meaning to your family.

Couples can make *tsedakah* an integral part of the *simcha* in a variety of ways, such as requesting contributions to designated charities in lieu of wedding presents, or donating money to charity in lieu of floral centerpieces or giving the flowers to a hospital or nursing home after the event.

A growing number of Jewish families and congregations happily donate 3 percent of food costs at all their *simchas* to Mazon (the Hebrew word for food). Mazon, A Jewish Response to Hunger, funds soup kitchens, food pantries, and a wide variety of nonprofit programs in the United States and around the world. Although Jewish tradition teaches that *tsedakah* is best given anonymously, an announcement of a Mazon contribution in the wedding booklet or a request for donations from guests might encourage guests to make a contribution on another joyful occasion. And that would be yet another *mitzvah*. (Mazon, 12401 Wilshire Boulevard, Suite 303, Los Angeles, CA 90025, 310-442-0020. www.mazon.org.)

A NOTE ON REMARRIAGE

The Jewish injunction "It is not good to be alone" makes every marriage a cause for celebration. The ceremony for widows, widowers, and divorced people is exactly the same as that for first-time marriages, and while Jewish law mandates three days of celebration after a second marriage (there are seven after the first), there is no reason for a second wedding to be the quiet, family-only affair once dictated by secular etiquette. Especially now that remarriage is an everyday phenomenon in the Jewish community, brides and grooms and their families should feel free to plan their weddings as they wish.

Remarriage may, however, pose some special challenges. Death or divorce doesn't necessarily sever ties to a first spouse's family. Widows, widowers, and divorced people often remain close to in-laws from their first marriages, especially if there are grandchildren. A first spouse's family may view a remarriage as a great blessing or they may feel it as a second loss. Obviously, the decision about whether or not to invite people who were once family depends on your relationship with them. Their feelings, as well as the wishes of your bride or groom and children, should be taken into account. Though it's not always possible, it is best for the situation to be discussed openly with everyone concerned.

Children from previous marriages may be included in wedding ceremonies in ways appropriate to their ages and emotional responses. Since the remarriage of a parent can be a difficult and confusing event, a child who is reluctant to participate should never be forced to walk down the aisle just because it would look "nice" or be reassuring to the parent and soon-to-be stepparent. Most rabbis will suggest at least one prewedding meeting with the bride, groom, and their children to discuss family dynamics as well as ceremonial roles.

Very young children can be part of the processional and/or asked to carry important ritual objects: rings, cups, or unlit candles to the *huppah.* Older children might read part of the ceremony: the opening prayer, the first kiddush, or one of the seven marriage blessings. Or they might select a poem or even write something to recite under the canopy. Teenage or grown children can hold *huppah* poles. Since all weddings "marry" more than the bride and groom, rabbis sometimes invite the couple's children under the *huppah* for a blessing on the new family.

PART THREE

CELEBRATIONS
AND RITUALS

BEFORE THE WEDDING

TENAIM: CELEBRATING ENGAGEMENT

The decision to marry is one of life's momentous choices. Some couples have made it the occasion for a celebration based on the Ashkenazic custom of *tenaim*—literally, the "conditions" of the marriage. Every engagement announces that two people are changing their status; the public declaration of their decision instantly designates them bride and groom. *Tenaim* kicks off the season of the wedding, officially and Jewishly.

From the twelfth to the early nineteenth century, *tenaim* announced that two families had come to terms on a match between their children. The document setting out their agreement, also called *tenaim,* would include the dowry and other financial arrangements, the date and time of the *huppah,* and a *knas*—or penalty, if either party backed out of the deal.

After the document was signed and read aloud by an esteemed guest, a piece of crockery was smashed. The origins of this practice are not clear; the most common interpretation is that a shattered dish recalls the destruction of the Temple in Jerusalem, and it is taken to demonstrate that a broken engagement cannot be mended. The broken dish also anticipates the shattered glass that ends the wedding ceremony. In some communities it was customary for all the guests to bring some old piece of crockery to smash on the floor. There is also a tradition that the mothers-in-law-to-be break the plate—a symbolic rending of mother-child ties and an acknowledgment that soon their children will be feeding each other.

Tenaím is not required by Jewish law, and as family-arranged weddings became a thing of the past, the ceremony lost much of its meaning and popularity. The signing of traditional *tenaim* remains a vestigial practice in some traditional Jewish communities, where the agreement to marry is signed on the day of the wedding itself. Modern reinterpretations of the *tenaim* return the ceremony to its original, anticipatory celebration some months in advance.

A celebration of your decision to marry doesn't require that anything be put on paper at all, but some couples have used this occasion to formalize decisions about their married life, including even specific subjects, such as money management, job decisions in a two-career household, moving to another part of the country or making *aliyah* (settling in Israel), raising children, and agreeing to counseling in case of difficulties. While this may sound very untraditional, in fact, *tenaim* documents have historically included clauses and amendments that reflected current and personal concerns.

Contemporary *tenaim* documents can be written in Hebrew and English, or just in English. New *tenaim* tend to be idiosyncratic and original and are a wonderful opportunity to create something entirely your own within a Jewish framework. The document can be typed, handwritten or written in calligraphy. You can share the contents with guests at an engagement party or keep them for just the two of you. Or you can use the occasion for a slightly different purpose: write letters to one another, speaking of your love, your goals for your marriage, whatever you wish to say. Then exchange these letters, perhaps at the party, but open them the night before the wedding, when many couples spend the evening apart.

A party to announce the news of a Jewish wedding can be simple or elaborate, formal or casual. Modern *tenaim* celebrations often involve improvisational rituals, sometimes structured around recognizable Jewish symbols, sometimes rooted in family traditions, and sometimes altogether original. Some examples of creative *tenaim* celebrations follow.

An Engagement-Party Tenaím. A close friend decided to give Anna and Jon a party to celebrate their upcoming wedding. After wine and cake, everyone gathered in the living room, where Anna explained a little about the history of *tenaim* and "formally" announced the date—according to both the Jewish and secular calendars—time, and location of the wedding. She said, "There we will read our *ketubah,* hear the seven wedding blessings, exchange rings, and break a glass."

Jon explained a little of the history of the wedding ceremony and said, "Anna and I are choosing to sanctify a new stage of our lives. It's not something we take lightly, and it's not something we can do all by ourselves." He explained: "You will all be witnesses to our wedding. The Hebrew word for witness, *ayd,* comes from the word *od,* which means 'duration.' A witness is someone who perceives an event, retains it in his or her memory, and gives permanence to what is transitory." [1]

The designated best man made a sentimental toast and then repeated the blessing over wine. A pottery bowl, bought expressly for the occasion, was placed inside an old pillowcase, and a special friend was asked to stamp on it. There were shouts of "Mazel tov!"

Later, a friend asked Anna and Jon to sit in the center of a circle of the guests. She produced scissors and a ball of colored yarn and asked each person to attach himself or herself to the couple and to tell the story of where and when they'd met, what they had learned from one another, and what the nature of the connection was. After an hour the room looked like a colorful, crazy spider's web. And friends from the different corners of Jon and Anna's lives had become a community that assembled again to rejoice at their wedding.

A Havdalah Tenaím. [2] Barbara's and Brian's education plans prevented them from marrying as soon as they would like, so they decided to make an agreement, in the presence of witnesses, that they would marry "in accordance with the law of Moses and Israel" within twelve months of their residing in the same household. They promised that until such time they would support and care for each other, visit and communicate as often as possible, and in case of a serious personal problem, they would attempt a reconciliation. They wrote this agreement in Hebrew and in English, with room for their signatures and the signatures of two witnesses.

They sent invitations to friends and family to come and celebrate their *tenaim*. The invitations included an explanation of the ceremony and a quote from Hosea 2:19: "I will betroth you forever. I will betroth you with righteousness and justice and with goodness and mercy."

The event was structured around *havdalah*, the ceremony on Saturday evening that separates Shabbat from the rest of the week and that celebrates distinctions. After Barbara explained the history of *tenaim*, she lit two separate candles rather than the customary braided *havdalah* candle. Brian talked about the contract they had drawn up, and then a friend told a Midrash about how Jacob and Rachel fell in love and made a pact that someday they would marry, no matter what happened to them. "And so the Bible says that Jacob served seven years for Rachel and they seemed to them but a few days because of their love for one another."

Barbara explained that at this *havdalah* she and Brian were making a distinction between a time when they were separate and a time when they would be together. The blessing over wine was sung and translated, and the couple dipped their ring fingers in the wine and put them to each other's lips. The wine was then passed to the people around them.

The witnesses read the *tenaim* document, and it was signed. The *havdalah* blessing traditionally recited over a spice box was pronounced over two fragrant blossoms Brian and Barbara gave to each other as tokens of *kinyan*, which were then passed around the room.

The guests were invited to add their thoughts and blessings, and then the couple took the two candles and together read, "As we bring together the two candles of our lives until this moment, we ask that our bond be as vibrant and as illuminating as this flame, that it continually be renewed by the strengths of our individual selves, and that like this powerful flame, our life together may bring light and warmth and service to our people." They brought the light of their two candles together and recited the blessing over the flame and a final *havdalah* prayer:

> *Blessed be You, Life-Spirit of the universe,*
> *Who makes a distinction between holy and not yet holy,*
> *between light and darkness,*
> *between Shabbat and the six days of the week,*
> *between committed and uncommitted,*
> *between common goals and personal goals,*
> *between love and aloneness.*
> *Blessed be you,*
> *Who distinguishes between what is holy,*
> *and what is not yet holy.*

Some wine was poured into a plate, and the candles were doused together in the wine. The plate was wrapped in a cloth and broken against a wall to shouts of "Mazel tov!" The *Shehehiyanu,* a prayer of thanksgiving, was sung. And the party went on into the night.

The pieces of the broken plate from this evening were mounted and framed and hang in Barbara and Brian's home.

Family Tenaím. Ruth and David gathered their large, extended clans for the announcement of their engagement. The news had long been anticipated and it was greeted with kisses and questions. Where? When? How?

After the initial hubbub died down, Ruth and David asked everyone to be seated. Because they came from very traditional homes, Ruth and David agreed that only a traditional *ketubah* would ensure peace during the months of planning. But they had taken the opportunity of writing *tenaim* that spelled out what they saw as their obligations to each other. They agreed to share equally in the raising of children and in the support of their family, and they also promised their best attempts at patience and understanding. David made special provision for a rabbi to act on his behalf to grant his wife a *get*—a religious divorce—in case he was, for any reason, unable to give Ruth a divorce himself. They read these *tenaim* to their families, who were both impressed and a little mystified by the seriousness of their children.

Ruth unwrapped a bowl she had saved from her childhood, and David produced a ceramic cup that was his since he was a baby. They explained the custom and asked their mothers to break them, which both women did, crying and laughing. Everyone was invited to take a little piece of broken bowl or cup as a memento of the evening.

Then Ruth and David distributed paper and pens to the people in the room and asked them to write a wish, or blessing, or memory, or any kind of message to each of them. They sealed these in envelopes, which they opened in the hour they spent alone, separately, before the *huppah.*

Finally, one of Ruth's sisters announced her plan to weave a *huppah* for the couple. She brought out rolls of wide pastel-colored ribbon, directed everyone where to stand and when to move, and created a canopy that shimmered like a rainbow.

The *huppah* hangs suspended over Ruth and David's bed. The letters from their family members—some of whom have died since their wedding—fill a treasured album.

Celebrating Community

Few marriages are "accomplished" in a single ceremony. From *tenaim* to *huppah,* brides and grooms inhabit a kind of celebratory never-never land filled with special meals and parties. These are occasions for affirming commitments we often take for granted, for celebrating with the different communities we inhabit and depend on.

Celebrating Sisterhood. For women in most cultures, marriage has been life's most important rite of passage. The gathering of women to celebrate with, adorn, and advise a bride before her wedding is probably as ancient a custom as marriage itself.

In Sephardic and Mizrachi communities, women's parties remain an important feature of wedding festivities. Specifics vary from community to community but, in general, sometime during the week before the *huppah* the female relations and friends of the bride (and depending on local practice, the groom's mother, sisters, and aunts) gather to eat, celebrate, and sing to the bride. The songs tend to be playful, romantic, and erotic. The food is abundant, elaborate, and mostly sweet. In some Middle-Eastern Jewish communities the bride's hands and feet are painted with a reddish paste made of henna (a cosmetic dye known to the ancient Eygptians) as protection against the evil eye. The bride is also ritually fed seven times by her mother—a gift of strength, an omen of abundance.

All that remains of women's wedding celebrations in America is the bridal shower, usually a literal showering of household goods: kitchen utensils and linens that essentially "dower" the bride. But toasters and tea towels need not be the only pretext for women to celebrate together. A shower can be an affirmation of sustaining women-to-women relationships in families and among friends—with or without the toasters. When gifts are handmade or representative of feelings and wishes for the bride, bridal showers can take on new meaning.

Whatever the nature of the gifts, the hostess(es) of the shower can create a powerful and beautiful event in any number of ways: each woman could be asked to bring a copy of a photograph of herself with the bride, which might be pasted into a commemorative scrapbook of the occasion. Or an instant-picture camera can snap each guest with the bride, and these could form a souvenir album.

Kitchen showers can feature family-secret or all-time-favorite recipes. A request could be made for kosher dishes or special foods served during Jewish holidays or the bride's favorites—from chocolate to Chinese cuisine. These, too, could be assembled in an album or card file.

Drawing inspiration from the American friendship quilt, the hostess(es) can ask each guest to make a quilt square decorated with a design that has some meaning for the bride or that conforms, perhaps, to a particular color scheme. Be sure to designate the size and shape of each piece and allow enough time for preparation. The squares can be sewn together—maybe even at the shower—to be used as the *huppah* cover and/or as a bedcovering. Extra or late-arriving squares can be used to create a challah cover, wall hanging, or pillow.

Whatever the theme or project, each woman can speak about her relationship with the bride, recalling the first time she met the bride's fiancé, and express her fondest wish for the couple's future. A recording of these words is a treasure.

Although *mikvah* is an essentially personal experience, it can also be the occasion for a very special women's party. It is customary among Sephardic women to celebrate the bridal *mikvah*. Musicians are hired to accompany the bride and a singing entourage of female family members and friends to and from the ritual bath.*

Men's Parties. Sephardic and Mizrachi men gather for male-only celebrations that mirror the women's festivities during the week prior to a wedding. Men, sometimes representing three or four generations, eat, sing, and tease the groom. In some Ashkenazic shtetls exuberant friends would carry wedding-bound compatriots through the streets and into the synagogue. Grooms were seated on the *bimah* (platform or altar) under a canopy, and special songs were sung in their honor.†

Stag parties and smokers came into vogue in Jewish communities as the ghetto walls crumbled and customs of the larger culture were adopted. Bachelor parties are infamous for rowdy excess and have not be-

---

* See "River from Eden" in the section "Spiritual Preparation" for a discussion of *mikvah* celebrations.

† The groom's table (in Yiddish, *chossen's tish*), which takes place immediately before the wedding ceremony, is another traditional men-only gathering. It is discussed in the section "The Wedding Day."

come fixtures of Jewish American life. Today, however, some grooms gather with male friends and relatives to ponder the meaning of marriage and fatherhood over food and drink. Men who go to *mikvah* before their weddings sometimes bring male friends with them to witness and help rejoice in that *mitzvah* as well.

Family Parties. When marriages were arranged, the parents of the couple learned a good deal about one another before agreeing to a match. Today, of course, parents are generally presented with their prospective in-laws as a fait accompli. The relationship between the parents of a married couple is a delicate but important thing. Hebrew and Yiddish languages recognize this by giving that relationship a unique name: *machetunim.*

Whenever and however your two sets of parents meet, the level of anxiety is bound to be high. Will they like us? Will we like them? Will we have anything in common? Parents are often even more anxious than the bride and groom. After all, they have been anticipating this event since before your birth.

Since first impressions can set the tone for a lifetime of family relations, planning for the first meeting is important. Whatever the size or setting of your first family get-togethers, the primary goal is to soften the boundaries between "your" side and "my" side.

One great way to accomplish this is to ask family members to bring photographs of your childhood. As parents share memories of first teeth, first bicycles, and first dates, they may discover that they have more than enough in common to "sit down at the table together," which is the traditional "prayer" for prospective *machetunim.*

If the wedding is to be held on Sunday, and if the bride and groom have decided against a week-long separation, a Friday-night Shabbat family dinner can begin the festivities on a very warm note. Both mothers can be asked to light Shabbat candles, both fathers to bless the wine, and grandparents can make the *motzi* blessing over challah. If the family dinner is held on the Saturday night preceding a Sunday wedding, a beautiful way of beginning the celebration is by making *havdalah*, the ceremony that marks the end of Shabbat.

A traditional and very effective icebreaker is singing. In the shtetl the prenuptial party was called *zmires*, or songs, and wedding musicians were hired to play then as well as after the *huppah*. Some families have a tradition of writing humorous lyrics to popular songs for family occasions, and the bride and groom expect to be melodically "roasted," with special attention paid to how they met, their shared interests, and their not-shared interests. The bride and groom can also write songs about their families, about how the printer messed up the invitations, about the trials and tribulations of renting a dance floor, et cetera. Songs don't have to be "Jewish"; camp songs, show tunes, anything catchy will do.

At a sizable family gathering a master of ceremonies can also be very helpful in loosening people up with jokes and toasts. (The tradition of the *badchan*, or wedding jester, is described in the section "Laughter, Music, and Dance.") The emcee at a family party can encourage toasts and blessings, and roasting and singing from both sides, and, finally, announce when the party is over and it's time to leave.

Another way of forging bonds between families is through the ceremonial presentation of special gifts. Although the giving of wedding gifts is thought of mostly as the obligation of guests, for many centuries grooms and brides and their families exchanged presents, prescribed by local custom, as a way of welcoming a new son or daughter into the family. Gifts such as these commonly have some part to play in the wedding and/or for the couple's Jewish life together: candlesticks for Shabbat, a kiddush cup, challah cover, a Seder plate, and works of art with Jewish themes.

In some communities men didn't wear a *tallis* until after marriage, so a traditional gift is for the bride and/or her parents to give the groom a prayer shawl. Since many women wear *tallesim*, a prayer shawl may be a thoughtful gift for the bride from her groom and his family. Families might even collaborate on hers-and-his *tallesim*. A *huppah* made of the *tallis* given by a bride to her groom, a groom to his bride, or by the two families to "their" children adds a personal dimension to the canopy, which symbolizes the new home being established.

A *tallis* can be commissioned by a weaver or handmade in one of a number of simple ways. You can, for example, just purchase a beautiful piece of cloth (traditionally either wool or linen and, according to Leviticus, never a combination of the two), hem it, and then attach the ritual fringes, or *tzitzit*. It is the fringes that transform a four-cornered piece of fabric into a *tallis*. A simple piece of fabric can be embroidered or appliquéd with a design of your choosing. If you purchase a *tallis*, a personalized *atarah*—literally, "crown"—or neckpiece, can be embroidered with a blessing, the name of the groom or bride, or a decorative design.[3]

Rehearsal Dinners. Some rabbis advise against this custom, and some even refuse to take part in wedding rehearsals. They report that it is a time-consuming, usually stressful, and virtually unnecessary step. Besides, the moment a bride and groom enter the *huppah* is unique, one that cannot and should not be practiced. The ceremony itself is very simple, and the order of processionals and recessionals can easily be left to the care of a wedding accomodator or to a trusted friend who will not be walking down the aisle and can act as the processional "starter." (The rabbi will give that person the cue for things to begin, and then she/he can direct mothers, fathers, attendants, groom, and bride to enter at the proper time.) In this way the dinner that should be helping cement the relationships between families can be free of the inevitable tensions that arise when already nervous people are ordered to march up and down the aisle.

Community Recognition. Like every life-cycle event, a wedding is celebrated on three levels: personal, familial, and communal. The impact of a marriage on the couple and their families is obvious; however, every marriage changes the whole Jewish community by creating a new family and also, in many cases, by offering the promise of new life.

The Jewish community publicly recognizes and congratulates its couples with a congregational "group hug" known as the *ufruf* (or *aufruf,* or *oyfruf,* depending on your Yiddish pronunciation). In the past, the honor was limited to the groom who, on the Shabbat before his wedding, was given the honor of the first *aliyah*—the first blessings before the Torah reading. Not even a bar mitzvah could take precedence over a groom, who would be pelted by candy, nuts, and raisins as he descended from the *bimah* (podium.)

In most congregations today, both the bride and groom are called up together, where they may share the blessings over one *parasha*—Torah portion. Some couples study the Torah portion and present a *d'var Torah*—an explication of the text they read. The rabbi then expresses the community's good wishes for the couple and sometimes repeats the blessing called *Mi She'beirakh.*[4] Candy is thrown at the two of them as they leave the *bimah.*

One congregation crafted a special blessing for the couple at an *ufruf.* Spoken by the whole community rather than the rabbi, it replaces the traditional *Mi She'beirakh:*

May the One who blessed the marriages of Sarah and Abraham, Rebecca and Isaac, Leah and Jacob and Rachel, bless the forthcoming marriage of _____ and _____ .

As two vines sharing a stake grow together, May your lives become joyfully intertwined.

May this union allow the Divine Spirit to shine more brightly within each of you.

May we, your friends and your community, support and nourish your relationship, fostering the growth of your love and understanding, your compassion and wisdom.

May the fruits of your labor always be sweet, and may we be able to continue to share in your joy.

Blessed are You, Adonai, Our God, Ruler of the Universe, who has kept us alive, sustained us, and enabled us to reach this season.[5]

—Sharon Hausman Cohen and Janet Elis Milder

After the service one or both of the families (traditionally, the groom's) provide a special kiddush, which may consist of wine and cake, or a luncheon for a small number of invited guests or the entire congregation. If the wedding is scheduled for the following day and there is a family dinner to attend that evening, this kiddush tends to be brief so that people have time to rest. But if the *ufruf* takes place a week before the wedding, the kiddush can be a joyous Shabbat-afternoon celebration, with eating and singing until *havdalah.*

Another way of including a whole congregation in the celebration of your wedding is to host an *Oneg Shabbat* after Friday-night services. Generally, an *Oneg* is a brief, informal affair that consists of coffee, cake, and schmoozing.

Spiritual Preparation

Jewish tradition considers marriage a turning point that gives people the opportunity to begin their lives anew, reborn as pure and as full of promise as Adam and Eve, the first bride and groom. The spiritual preparation for marriage is very much like the intense reflection and soul-searching of Yom Kippur, when all sins are forgiven those who repent or make *t'shuva*—those who literally turn away from error and arrogance to begin the new year with a clean slate.

The fact that weddings are a very private encounter between two individuals and what they consider holy often gets lost in the onslaught of decisions and details that surround the public event. This chapter includes some traditional and not so traditional ways of letting go of the details of the public event and of considering the meaning of the private encounter.

Mikvah. The River from Eden

For centuries the Jewish bride has immersed herself in a *mikvah*—a ritual bath—in preparation for her wedding. The bridal *mikvah* was a woman's first trip to a place that would be part of her married life's rhythms for as long as she menstruated, and for traditional Jews *mikvah* remains a crucial part of married life.*

Fundamentally, *mikvah* is not about "uncleanness" but about human encounters with the power of the holy.[7] The Torah prescribes immersion not only for women after menstruation but also for men after seminal emissions. The scribe who works on a Torah scroll must immerse himself before writing God's name. All converts to Judaism are required to immerse themselves in the *mikvah*, marking their rebirth as members of the people of Israel. Some Jews—both men and women—go to *mikvah* in preparation for Yom Kippur, when one has the opportunity to begin the year with a pure heart.

According to the Talmud, the ultimate source of all water is the river that emerged from Eden.[8] By immersing themselves in the *mikvah*, people participate in the wholeness of Eden and are reborn. *Mikvah* also represents the physical source of life—the womb—from which humans enter the world untouched by sin.

For brides and grooms *mikvah* is a physical enactment of the passage from being unmarried to married. Entering the *huppah* is a public declaration of a change in status; entering the *mikvah* is a private transforming moment. Metaphorically, immersion creates newborns—virgins—so *mikvah* can be seen as the demarkation between premarital and married sexuality.

A *mikvah* is any body of *mayyim hayyim*, literally, "living water," running water as opposed to stagnant water. Ponds, lakes, rivers, and seas are natural *mikvaot*. For many, *mikvah* in a body of natural water is a more satisfying experience—spiritually, emotionally, and aesthetically—than *mikvah* indoors in what looks like a miniature swimming pool.

---

*During her menstrual flow and for seven days after, a woman is *niddah*—from the word *naddad*, which means "separated"—and she and her husband abstain from sexual contact. After *mikvah* immersion a woman is no longer *niddah*, and she and her husband are permitted to approach each other again.[6]

However, weather, climate, or family custom often discourages outdoor *mikvah.*

The act of *mikvah* is very simple, involving two or three immersions in water and one blessing. You enter the water nude, relax arms and legs, and immerse yourself so that every strand of hair is underwater. The eyes should not be shut tightly. You duck under, looking and feeling like a fetus in the womb.

Upon rising from the water you repeat the blessing for immersion:

בָּרוּךְ אַתָּה יְיָ, אֱלֹהֵינוּ מֶלֶךְ הָעוֹלָם אֲשֶׁר קִדְּשָׁנוּ
בְּמִצְוֹתָיו, וְצִוָּנוּ עַל הַטְבִילָה.

Baruch ata Adonai Eloheynu Melech Ha-olam asher kid'shanu, be-mitzvotav vitsivanu al ha'tevilah.

Praised are you, Adonai, God of all creation, who sanctifies us with your commandments and commanded us concerning immersion.

Custom varies on the number of immersions: two are common but three are also traditional since the word *mikvah* appears three times in the Torah. Other prayers may, of course, be added. For brides and grooms the most common addition is the *Shehehiyanu,* the blessing commemorating significant first events:

בָּרוּךְ אַתָּה יְיָ, אֱלֹהֵינוּ מֶלֶךְ הָעוֹלָם. שֶׁהֶחֱיָנוּ וְקִיְּמָנוּ
וְהִגִּיעָנוּ לַזְּמַן הַזֶּה:

Baruch ata Adonai, Eloheynu Melech Ha-olam shehechiyanu vikiamanu vihigianu lazman hazeh.

Blessed are You, Adonai, Ruler of the Universe, who kept us alive and preserved us and enabled us to reach this season.

A traditional blessing for *mikvah* is the *Yehi Ratzon*, a prayer for the reestablishment of the Temple, a prayer envisioning a world as whole and pure as you hope to be upon emerging from *mikvah*:

יְהִי רָצוֹן מִלְּפָנֶיךָ יְיָ אֱלֹהֵינוּ וֵאלֹהֵי אֲבוֹתֵינוּ שֶׁיִּבָּנֶה
בֵּית הַמִּקְדָּשׁ בִּמְהֵרָה בְיָמֵינוּ. וְתֵן חֶלְקֵנוּ בְּתוֹרָתֶךָ. וְשָׁם
נַעֲבָדְךָ בְּיִרְאָה. כִּימֵי עוֹלָם וּכְשָׁנִים קַדְמוֹנִיּוֹת. וְעָרְבָה
לַיְיָ מִנְחַת יְהוּדָה וִירוּשָׁלָיִם כִּימֵי עוֹלָם וּכְשָׁנִים
קַדְמוֹנִיּוֹת.

May it be Your will, Adonai, our God and God of our parents, that the Temple be speedily rebuilt in our days, and grant our portion in Your Torah. There we will serve You with awe as in days of old and as in ancient years. And may the offerings of Judah and Jerusalem be as pleasant to You as ever and as in ancient times.

Most indoor *mikvaot* are maintained by Orthodox communities, though a growing number of Reform and Conservative synagogues operate them as well. Your rabbi should be able to direct you to the nearest one.

Although brides are sometimes allowed to use them free of charge or for a very nominal amount, most *mikvaot* depend on fees for use of the facilities in order to survive. Ask about the fee when you call to make an appointment. Men's hours are usually far more restricted, so grooms should call well in advance.

Most *mikvaot* employ an attendant who is universally known as "the *mikvah* lady," and if you've never been to *mikvah* before, it's easy to be intimidated by her. It's important to remember that her function is not to judge but simply to assist in the performance of a mitzvah. By and large, *mikvah* ladies ask no questions.

Although the immersions and blessings take only a few minutes, plan to spend an hour at the *mikvah*. You will be shown to a private bathroom, usually equipped with towels and perhaps even with disposable tooth-brushes, kosher toothpaste, shampoo, and hair dryers. (When you call for an appointment, ask what you need to bring.) The order of your ablu-tions is entirely up to you. Clean and trim finger- and toenails; clean ears and floss and brush your teeth. If the *mikvah* is not too crowded, soak and relax in the tub. Consider bringing some bubble bath and a facial mask. Then shower, shampoo your hair, and rinse thoroughly. Comb all the hair on your head and body in the same direction. There will be a towel or sheet for wrapping yourself before calling the *mikvah* lady.

She will lead you to the *mikvah* and inspect you to make sure you are ready to immerse. (This usually takes no more than a few seconds, and her businesslike demeanor precludes embarrassment.) She will then tell you to immerse yourself and will lead you through the blessings. If you know the prayers, you may be able to convince her that you know the procedure and don't need her supervision. Afterward you return to the bathroom to dress. (Of course there are male attendants during men's hours.)

If you decide to go to a traditional *mikvah*, preparation can make the difference between a relaxing, meaningful experience and a confusing, even alienating one. Before you leave for *mikvah* take some time to think about what the ritual means to you. Go for a walk with friends. Meditate.

Celebrating Mikvah. The Sephardic custom of turning *mikvah* into a joyful party has inspired new rituals and celebrations. These can be very simple, involving an intimate dinner for the bride or groom when she/he returns, or they can be as elaborate and creative as you like:

- One bride mystified the *mikvah* lady by arriving with five friends car-rying flowers and a basket filled with food and wine. They waited for her in the foyer, and when she returned after immersion, greeted her with songs, champagne, and her favorite sweets.
- One groom gathered his closest friends at an ocean beach on the morn-ing of his wedding. They sang and prayed as he plunged into the surf

and recited the blessing. When he emerged from the water everyone sang the *Shehehiyanu.* Together, singing, they accompanied the groom to his room to prepare for the *huppah.*

- A bride took her three sisters to a nearby pond the night before her wedding. They held big towels as she immersed herself in the water and sang the blessing. When she emerged in the moonlight each sister whispered a private wish for her happiness.

There are many ways to physically commemorate the entry of a bride or groom into a new stage in her/his life, observing the spirit, if not the letter, of the law:

- Although *mikvah* in a bathing suit lacks the symbolic power of nude immersion, it has been done. One group of women gathered on the far shore of a popular swimming hole a week before their friend's wedding. In a circle around the bride, they all immersed themselves. While still in the water each woman in turn wished for the water to wash away one of the bride's self-doubts. Then each one praised the bride for specific abilities, talents, and beauties. Similar *mikvah* celebrations have been held in private swimming pools and even in hot tubs. At one, each guest lit a floating candle with a personal wish for the bride's happiness.

- The ritual washing of hands and feet has been an important Jewish symbol for generations. In Genesis, Abraham washed the feet of the three angels who visited him at his tent, both as an act of welcome and as a token of his esteem. The daily mitzvah of hand washing in the morning and before eating symbolizes the removal of impurity and renewed spiritual integrity.

At one "*mikvah* gathering" for both the bride and groom, guests poured pure spring water over their hands. As each person poured, she/he offered a wish for the couple's future. The pitcher and bowl, bought especially for the occasion, were given to the couple as a wedding gift.

- In the spirit of "annointing," one wedding "queen" was seated on a special "throne," to which her closest women friends brought gifts of scent. Each one brought a pure distilled oil of a favorite fragrance—rose, musk, apple blossom, lemon, lily of the valley—and placed a drop on her wrist, her neck, or the inside of her elbow. Since smell is the most ethereal of our senses, the *havdalah* spice box is passed on Shabbat to offer a final reminder of the beauties of paradise. Covering the bride with reminders of paradise enacts wishes for a perfect marriage.

- Finally, a *mikvah* of song can be created for the prewedding purification of a sister or friend. A group of women arranged themselves in two lines. Humming softly, they raised their arms to form a kind of passageway between them. As the singing grew louder, and when she felt ready, the bride made her way slowly through this birth canal of sound. At the end of the passageway, which was also a bridge, she washed her face and hands from a bowl of water.[9]

Prayers for Mikvah. From the sixteenth to the nineteenth century, hundreds of books full of women's prayers called *techinnes* or *tehinnot* were published in Europe. These were mainly petitionary prayers filled with the concerns of daily life and the life cycle of women. There is a *tehinnah* to recite if a child should fall sick, one for an orphan to say on her wedding day, and another to repeat after giving birth.[10]

Tehinnot were also written for *mikvah.* The following prayers, excerpted from a bridal *mikvah* ceremony written by Barbara Rosman Penzner and Amy Small, are modern *tehinnot,* a bridge to the generations of women who preceded us into the water.

> *Now, as I immerse myself,*
> *I begin a new cycle,*
> *a cycle of rebirth and renewal*
> *of Your world and Your people Israel.*
> *I prepare for my new life*
> *and for the sanctification of that life*
> *through kiddushin . . .*

Our mothers Rebekkah and Rachel
were betrothed and began new lives
at the gently flowing water of the well.
Our mother Yochevet
gave life to her child Moses in the
ever-flowing waters of the Nile.
Our sister Miriam
danced for the saving of lives
beside the
overflowing water
of the Sea of Reeds.

Water is God's gift to living souls,
to cleanse us, to purify us,
to sustain and to renew us.

As Moses and Aaron
and the priests of Israel
washed with cleansing waters
before attending to God's service
at the altar,
So I now cleanse myself
before Your altar of sanctification.

I am now prepared to shed
the impurities of my earlier life;
to become one with another life,
to become a creator of new life,
to become a partner in sharing the joys of life,
to teach and to learn
the lessons of married life.[11]

The Memory of the Righteous Is a Blessing

If a bride or groom has lost one or both parents, tradition suggests a prewedding visit to the grave(s) of the dead. Far from being maudlin, this practice can be very healing and cathartic at a time when a loss can seem especially keen. "If only she/he had lived long enough to see this . . ."

During the exhilaration of getting ready, there may be twinges of sadness, even guilt, about not mourning a dead relative or intimate friend who would have so loved to dance at your wedding. Taking the time to visit the grave gives the mourner a chance to remember the loss and to forgive him/herself.

If you decide to visit the cemetery, you might wish to take along your spouse-to-be as a way of bringing him/her closer to the person she/he will never get to know. This can be both a way of giving life to your memories and of sharing a part of yourself. If you are afraid words may fail you, bring a poem your parent liked or something that reminds you of him or her. Tell your fiancé(e) a favorite story about your parent or a story she/he liked to tell about you. If the grave is too far away to visit, set aside some time for reminiscing, leaf through a family photo album, listen to some of his/her favorite music—alone or with your partner.

There are other kinds of losses that tend to lack religious or social forms of acknowledgment. For people who have been married and divorced and for people whose histories include other important intimate relationships, it can be useful to take time to mourn the formal end of those loves as well.

> *You are remembered in love.*
> *You are part of the now in me.*
> *All the good*
> *All the love*
> *All the comfort a person can give*
> *Is remembered*
> *And repeated*

For your sake.
Time changes
Everything passes
But love.
Peace abide you.[12]

Absence Makes the Heart . . .

As in many other cultures, it is customary for the bride and groom to be separated for some period of time before the wedding. Since the groom traditionally covers his bride with the veil before he sees her under the *huppah*, this seems less a matter of superstition among Jews than an occasion for serious reflection.

It was long the custom for couples to be apart for a week. Today, however, it's more common for the separation to last only a day or two. Some couples decide to stay apart from the time of *mikvah* until the wedding. (Such a decision obviously rules out prewedding dinners that include the entire wedding party.)

Some people who live together before marriage think the idea of separation is irrelevant if not dishonest, but others find it useful. Between family squabbles and the inevitable last-minute crises, the week before any wedding can cause serious friction between brides and grooms. A brief period of separation may be a welcome tension breaker. It can allow the bride and groom to spend a little private time with family members or friends who've come a long distance. It makes a little time to simply pause and reflect.

And even the briefest separation heightens anticipation. For Jews, ritual self-denial is not about the mortification of the flesh; the point of any fast is the enhanced enjoyment once it is time to eat—or in this case, meet—again.

Fasting

It is traditional for brides and grooms to fast on the wedding day. As on Yom Kippur, abstaining from food symbolizes a new start. It is said that the people of Israel fasted on the day that the Torah was given to them at Sinai, so bride and groom fast in preparation for their covenant with each other.

The couple break the fast together when they drink from the first cup of wine under the *huppah*. After the ceremony the two who began fasting separately, will feed each other their first meal as wife and husband, secluded in *yichud*.

Fasting is, however, prohibited on days of joy and semi-holidays, including: Rosh Hodesh, the holiday of the new moon, except Rosh Hodesh Nissan; Issru Chag, the day after the final days of Passover; Shavuot, Sukkot, Hanukkah, and Purim; the fifteenth day of Av; and the fifteenth day of Shevat. And rabbis sometimes discourage this custom if the wedding is set for eight or nine P.M. on a summer Saturday night.

Prayer

The prayers associated with weddings are an assorted lot; they include supplication that the caterer will get things right, thanks for having found such a wonderful partner, blessings for the future, and, traditionally, prayers of confession. This last category is part of the cleansing process that includes *mikvah* and fasting.

It is traditional for brides and grooms to repeat the Yom Kippur Viddui, a litany of sins that is chanted by the whole congregation on the Day of Atonement. The form of the Viddui ("We have sinned, we have transgressed") lends itself to personal and specific versions:

> *I have been quick to anger with my family and*
> *I have been afraid to show them my love.*
> *I have failed to listen to my teachers.*

I have spoken too loudly to my beloved.
I have hurt others.
I have allowed others to be hurt without reaching out to help.
I have lied to myself and to others.
I have forgotten my better self.

I turn to those I have hurt and ask their forgiveness.
I turn to those who have hurt me and forgive them.
I turn within and forgive myself. [13]

Another traditional prayer that seems especially relevant and sweet in preparation for a wedding is the *T'filat HaDerech,* a Prayer for Travelers, which is recited before undertaking a journey:

May it be Your will, before You,
Adonai our God and God of our ancestors,
to lead us in safety, to direct our steps in safety,
to guide us in safety,
and enable us to reach our destination
in life, in joy, and in peace,
and bring us back home in peace. [14]

The Wedding Day

Jewish wedding custom includes special ceremonies of greeting and preparation before the *huppah* is raised. Pre-*huppah* festivities also heighten anticipation and set the tone for the whole day.

Tradition gives us several such ceremonies: *kabbalat panim* (literally, "receiving faces"), which in Yiddish is *chossen's tish*—a gathering at the "groom's table"; *hakhnassat kallah*—attending or escorting the bride; *bedeken de kallah*—veiling the bride; and the *ketubah* signing.

All of the "pre-*huppah*" ceremonies described here can create momentum and *kavannah* (spiritual intention) building to the crescendo of the wedding itself. They can also provide ways to honor special family members and friends with honorary roles (pen bearer, veil carrier, etc.)

The Groom's Table. All the male guests (or just a small circle of friends and relatives) gather to sign *tenaim* and the *ketubah*. Before the *ketubah* can be signed, the rabbi or one of the witnesses must make a *kinyan*—the ritual act of acquisition—with the groom. Acting on behalf of the bride, the rabbi or one of the witnesses gives the groom some object, usually a handkerchief. By accepting it the groom indicates that he is willing to assume the obligations stipulated in the *ketubah*. Schnapps (whiskey) or wine and cake are served, and the groom may present a *d'var Torah*, a lecture on the weekly Torah portion. However, in order to spare the already nervous groom, he is invariably interrupted with songs and jokes from his guests.

Attending the Bride. While the groom and his friends are thus engaged, the bride is surrounded by women in another room. She may be seated in a special chair covered with pillows or perhaps a white sheet strewn with flowers to receive greetings and blessings from her guests. The women sing songs and dance around her chair, and the wedding musicians may make their first appearance here.

Veiling. When she is ready, the bride sends a delegation to the groom's table to invite the men to the veiling, which is the last ceremony before the wedding begins. This is usually the first time the bride and groom have seen each other for a week or a few days. The groom, attended by his guests, enters the bride's chamber, where she is flanked by members of her family or by both mothers. The groom lowers the veil over the bride's face to avoid making Jacob's mistake. Because he didn't see the face of his bride, Jacob married Leah instead of Rachel, the woman he loved (Genesis 29:23–25). By "dressing" his bride with a veil the groom also sets her apart from all others.

Ketubah Signing. Although it is a fundamentally legal transaction, the signing, like the document itself, can be very beautiful. Some couples invite all their guests to attend and act as witnesses. Others make an intimate time of this with a small group of family and friends only, and create a space for everyone to settle down, take a breath, and focus. Some rabbis suggest that this is a good time for publicly remembering loved ones who are no longer alive.

The vignettes that follow demonstrate the variety of ways that couples adapt traditional forms to suit their own, and their family's, needs and tastes.

Tish for Two. To begin their wedding Ellen and Mark decided to hold both a *chossen's tish* and a *kallah's tish*—bride's table. Male guests were directed to one room in the synagogue and women to another. Hors d'oeuvres, tea, and wine were served. At the *kallah's tish* Ellen's cousin delivered a short speech about the bride's family history, paying special attention to stories about her matrilineal relatives—grandmothers, aunts, sisters, and mother. At Mark's *tish* his best friend spoke about the meaning of the groom's Hebrew name, Moshe, which was also his great-grandfather's name.

Ellen decided not to wear a veil, so after the two "tables" the couple, their parents, and the two witnesses joined the rabbi in his study for the *ketubah* signing. Meanwhile, as a variation on the "guest book," the rest of the company was asked to write personal messages into a "book of blessings." A shofar blast called everyone into the sanctuary for the *huppah*.

A Lehrnen. Barbara and Brian invited their immediate family and closest friends to a pre-*huppah* gathering they called "the *lehrnen*"—Yiddish for "learning." People gathered around a table in the synagogue's function room, where cake and brandy were served. The couple spoke about the importance of mutuality in their wedding ceremony, and they explained why they had decided to use both a traditional and an egalitarian *ketubah.*

Next Barbara placed a *kippah* (yarmulke) on Brian's head. Brian draped the veil over Barbara, and they spoke the priestly blessing to each other. The rabbi explained the meaning of *kinyan,* after which both Barbara and Brian took hold of the kerchief he extended to them, symbolically yet actively consenting to all that was about to happen.

Two of their closest friends, a woman and a man, signed the marriage contracts. The rabbi led the group in some songs, and then family members and friends told stories about the couple until it was time for the ceremony to begin.

The Rose-Covered Kallah. Larry's *tish* conformed to the customs of his traditional family. He prepared a short *d'var Torah* on the Torah portion for the week of his wedding and delivered it to the applause of the male members of his large, extended family. The *ketubah* was signed by two male witnesses at the *chossen's tish,* after which there was something of a "roast," with song parodies and silly limericks about the groom.

Meanwhile Suri was in another room receiving the women guests. Each woman greeted Suri with a white rose. Every guest whispered her best wishes as she kissed the bride and placed her flower in one of the vases arranged around her chair. Eventually the bride was surrounded by flowers, which were later transferred to the tables at the wedding dinner.

As a memorial to an aunt who had died the year before, Suri placed above her bridal throne a canopy made of a fine lace tablecloth treasured by her aunt.

The groom was carried on a chair into Suri's room. As Larry lowered the veil, Suri's brother recited the traditional blessing:

אֲחֹתֵנוּ אַתְּ הֲיִי לְאַלְפֵי רְבָבָה.

Achotenu: at hayi le'alfei revavah.
Our sister, may you be the mother of thousands of myriads.

Finally, her father held his daughter's hands as he repeated the benediction:

> *May God make you like Sarah, Rebekkah, Rachel and Leah.*
> *May God bless you and keep you,*
> *May God make The Countenance shine upon you and be*
>   *gracious to you,*
> *May God lift The Countenance upon you and give you peace.*

Larry's brother helped him on with a *kittel,* and the guests proceeded to the sanctuary for the *huppah.*

Music and Dancing. Helen and Mark were fortunate in having many talented musicians among their friends. Mark and his male guests were serenaded with singing and guitar playing at the *chossen's tish* while women danced around Helen's chair to the sounds of flute, drum, and tambourine. Mark was brought to Helen by means of a singing conga line, which then circled the two of them.

A traditional *ketubah* was signed by two male and two female witnesses after Mark and Helen accepted a pen from the rabbi as *kinyan.* As Mark lowered the veil and Helen helped Mark into a *kittel* she had made, the musicians played a melody that became the theme of their wedding; the same tune was played as they walked to the *huppah,* and again to accompany their first dance together as husband and wife.

Meditative Moments. Judith and Alan, who had both been married before, decided on a small, at-home wedding. They chose to use the hours before their wedding for reflection and for talking with members of their families. Judith made fifteen-minute-long "appointments" with her mother, father, sister, and daughter. Alan went for a short walk with his parents. Then they met with the rabbi, who led them through a brief meditation.

Judith and Alan wanted their veiling to be an especially intimate event, when they could search each other's eyes before entering the *huppah*. Only the rabbi and the couple's immediate family were present when Alan covered Judith with the lace mantilla he had bought as a wedding gift. The rabbi then spoke of the mystical teachings about veiling: that it gives the bride "special eyes" with which to watch over her children, and that *bedeken* connects her to the future, so that when she walks to the *huppah*, all her children and grandchildren until the end of their generations walk with her.

When the guests arrived the rabbi read the *ketubah*, which was signed by the bride, groom, rabbi, and two official witnesses. All the guests were then invited to sign and become witnesses as well.

All Together Now. When Abby and Jacob were married, the pre-wedding festivities and *huppah* took place in the same room, in one continuous motion. The rabbi assembled all the guests around a table at one end of the sanctuary and taught them a *niggun*—a wordless melody. As they sang and clapped, Jacob followed his mother into the room. Next Abby followed her parents up to the table. The two witnesses were asked to come and sit with the bride, groom, and rabbi. The first of the two cups of wine was blessed and given to the couple to drink. Then the *ketubah* was explained, read aloud, and signed by the five people at the table. Abby removed the blue *kippah* from Jacob's head and replaced it with a new white one; Jacob put a veil on Abby.

The *huppah* pole holders were then instructed to raise the canopy, which had been readied in another part of the room, and the guests took their seats around it. Two musicians playing flute and guitar struck up a slow, stately version of a Yiddish folk song. The groom's mother walked to the *huppah* on the arm of the male witness; the bride's father followed with the female witness; and then the bride's mother and brother walked down the aisle. The bride and groom entered the *huppah* together and the ceremony began.

UNDER
THE HUPPAH

A Little History. Although some elements are much older, the Jewish wedding began to take its current shape during the eleventh century. Before that, marriage was accomplished in two distinct rituals, separated by as much as a year. The first of these was betrothal, or *erusin,* also called *kiddushin,* from the same root as the word *kadosh,* meaning "holy." After their betrothal the bride and groom were considered legally wed, and a *get,* the formal bill of divorce, was necessary to dissolve the contract. Even so, the marriage was not consummated until after the next ceremony, *nissuin*—"nuptials."

Nissuin derives from the verb *nasa,* which means "to carry or lift" and may refer to the days when a bride was carried through the streets to her new home. *Nissuin,* which also came to be called *huppah,* is accomplished by means of a symbolic act of intimacy that demonstrates the couple's intention to create a new home and new life. *Yichud* (seclusion) became the accepted way of proving that the bride and groom were now husband and wife.

The two ceremonies differ in function and feeling. *Kiddushin* is a legal contract involving the precise formulas and transactions of *ketubah* and *kinyan; nissuin* is a far less tangible process, sealed not with documents but with actions. Betrothal designates the bride and groom for each other only, but nuptials give them to each other. *Kiddushin* forges the connection between bride and groom; *nissuin,* which can also mean "elevation," connects husband and wife with God.

After nearly ten centuries and despite the fact that both *kiddushin* and *nissuin* are now carried out beneath the *huppah*, Jewish weddings still show the seam where the two ceremonies were joined. The presence of two cups (or one cup filled and blessed twice) is a reminder of the time when two separate occasions with two separate recitations of kiddush, the prayer of sanctification over wine.

The separation of *erusin/kiddushin* and *nissuin/huppah* came to an end during the eleventh century for a number of practical reasons. First, two separate ceremonies meant two separate banquets, which imposed financial difficulties on all but the wealthiest. Second, the Middle Ages were perilous times for Jews, and an intervening year might bring deportation or death to one of the parties. If a betrothed groom disappeared, his bride became *agunah*, a woman who was unable to marry. Finally, since many grooms lived with the bride's family before *huppah*, the ceremonies were combined to remove the obvious and understandable temptations of couples who had been promised to each other but were forbidden to touch.

Betrothal: The Ring Ceremony

Most Jewish weddings begin with two introductions. The first extends a welcome to the people gathered, especially the bride and groom. The second is a prayer for God's presence and blessing. Although neither the greeting nor the invocation is required by Jewish law, both have long histories in practice.

The Greetings. Spoken or chanted by the rabbi or cantor, the traditional greeting comes from Psalms 118:26:

בָּרוּךְ הַבָּא בְּשֵׁם יְיָ.

Baruch haba b'Shem Adonai
Welcome in the name of Adonai

בֵּרַכְנוּכֶם מִבֵּית יְיָ:

Berakhnukhem mi'beyt Adonai
Welcome in this house of Adonai

Since a *huppah* consecrates any place, the second line that refers to God's "house" is included even if the wedding is not held in a synagogue.

Some rabbis take this moment to remind the guests that their role at a Jewish wedding is not a passive one; they are obliged not only to rejoice and honor the bride and groom on their wedding day but also to remain a sustaining community for them. Since it is believed that the relationship of bride and groom increases the potential for peace and holiness in the world, rabbis sometimes offer a prayer that the wedding will prove to be a source of blessing for all of humanity.

Invocation. Once the guests have been welcomed, God is asked to bless the wedding. The rabbi or cantor will recite or chant words that "call down" particular aspects of the Divine, usually with the prayer called *Mi Adir:*

מִי אַדִּיר עַל הַכֹּל.
מִי בָּרוּךְ עַל הַכֹּל.
מִי גָּדוֹל עַל הַכֹּל.
יְבָרֵךְ אֶת־הֶחָתָן וְאֶת־הַכַּלָּה

Mi Adir el hakol,
Mi Baruch el hakol
Mi Gadol el hakol
Ye'varesh hahatan v'hakallah.

Splendor is upon everything
Blessing is upon everything
Who is full of this abundance
Bless this groom and bride.[15]

Blessing for the First Cup. There is a saying "Without wine there is no blessing." Wine is associated with celebrations, festivals, and *simcha*—joy. Kiddush is part of virtually all Jewish observance as a prayer of sanctification. Although it is acceptable to use a single goblet that is re-filled and counted twice, it is common to use two cups, which are placed on a small table under the canopy.

These kiddush cups provide another opportunity for *hiddur mitzvah* and personal symbolism. The old European custom of creating a special wedding cup or a matched pair of goblets has been revived by Jewish artisans. Goblets used during the ceremony can become household ritual objects and family heirlooms. Some couples take time to shop for a particularly beautiful cup or two, others use kiddush cups that have been a part of their families' observance.

Although the couple may chant the blessing, it is customary for the rabbi or cantor to chant kiddush on their behalf, and for the couple to respond with an "amen."

בָּרוּךְ אַתָּה יְיָ אֱלֹהֵינוּ מֶלֶךְ הָעוֹלָם, בּוֹרֵא פְּרִי הַגָּפֶן:

> *Baruch ata Adonai Eloheynu Melech Ha-olam, borey p'ree ha-gaffen.*
>
> *Holy One of the Blessing, Your presence fills creation, forming the fruit of the vine.*

In most cases the wine is not drunk until after *birkhat erusin*—the blessings of betrothal.

Birkat Erusin: The Betrothal Blessings. Since this blessing was once recited a full year before *nissuin,* it included a very specific warning to betrothed couples (the groom in particular) that they are not permitted to approach each other sexually until after the second ceremony:

בָּרוּךְ אַתָּה, יְיָ אֱלֹהֵינוּ, מֶלֶךְ הָעוֹלָם, אֲשֶׁר קִדְּשָׁנוּ
בְּמִצְוֹתָיו, וְצִוָּנוּ עַל הָעֲרָיוֹת, וְאָסַר לָנוּ אֶת הָאֲרוּסוֹת,
וְהִתִּיר לָנוּ אֶת הַנְּשׁוּאוֹת לָנוּ עַל יְדֵי חֻפָּה וְקִדּוּשִׁין.

Praised are you Adonai, Ruler of the universe, who has made us holy through Your commandments and has commanded us concerning sexual propriety, forbidding to us (women) who are merely betrothed, but permitting to us (women) who are married to us through *huppah* and *kiddushin*. Blessed are You, Adonai, who makes Your people Israel holy through *huppah* and *kiddushin*.

This blessing tends to be translated and interpreted in a far less specific manner regarding *kiddushin* and *nissuin*, often along the lines of ". . . and has commanded us concerning marriages that are forbidden and those that are permitted when carried out under the canopy and with the sacred wedding ceremonies."

Some rabbis read the Hebrew *b'racha* and substitute an English prayer that is only loosely based on the original, for example:

You are Holy, Adonai, and Your presence permeates the universe. Through your commandments we share your holiness. You teach us to rejoice with the bride and groom, to celebrate their consecration to each other, to witness their vows to each other, here beneath the bridal canopy. You are Holy, Adonai, and you sanctify the union of Your children beneath the canopy.[16]

or

Praised are You, Adonai our God, who has allowed us to share life through *huppah* and marriage. Praised are you God, who sanctifies your people Israel through the covenant of marriage.

or

Blessed be the Infinite, lifting us up through holy celebration and awakening us to seek love and to sanctify our love through *huppah* and marriage. Blessed be the Infinite, making the Jewish people and all who dwell in the world holy through holy weddings.[17]

After this blessing, the wine is drunk. There is some rabbinical debate about who should drink from the cup. Sometimes the rabbi will take a sip and then hand the cup first to the groom and then to the bride, but generally only the bride and groom drink. Sharing from the same cup carries the obvious interpretation that married life halves bitterness, doubles sweetness.

This sip of wine often provokes a tear for parents who remember another cup of wine. For centuries, the celebration of a son's *bris* (ritual circumcision) has included giving the baby a drop of wine, and reciting a prayer that his life will include study of Torah, the marriage canopy, and good works. The same sweet sense of completion now also applies to daughters as well as sons, since covenant and naming ceremonies for girls also incorporate a drop of wine in the baby's mouth, and the same three-fold prayer—for Torah, *huppah, v' ma'asim tovim*. From one covenant to the next, from one cup to the next, the taste of wine under the *huppah* fulfills this prayer.

If at this point the bride is wearing a veil that covers her face, it is lifted so she can drink. This can be a special honor, performed either by the mothers of the bride and groom or by an attendant. If the bride did not give her bouquet to an attendant before entering the *huppah,* she will hand it to someone before taking the cup.

In some communities the first cup of wine is shared with members of the immediate family and sometimes with close friends. The rabbi or an attendant may carry the cup to grandparents, who are seated close to the *huppah*. Or the bride will hold the cup for her future in-laws, and the groom will do the same for his.

The sharing of wine with others may be publicly acknowledged by the rabbi:

> *Two cups are before you. By your choice, only one is reserved for the two of you alone. You decided to share the first cup with those who have been partners in your lives thus far, the ones who have helped to make you the individuals you are.*
>
> *We are grateful to you, Source of all Creation, for the loving care and teaching of parents, the ties of heart and mind and memory that link brothers and sisters, and for the friendships that fill our cup to overflowing.*[18]

The Ring Ceremony. The groom's giving and the bride's acceptance of a ring is the central act of *kiddushin*. With the ring the groom accomplishes *kinyan* and "acquires" the bride. Strictly speaking, the groom is supposed to memorize the marriage formula, but in order to spare him any embarrassment the rabbi says the words, which the groom then repeats. Because it is essential that both bride and groom understand the meaning of these words, the statement is recited both in Hebrew and English (or whatever language the couple knows best):

הֲרֵי אַתְּ מְקֻדֶּשֶׁת לִי בְּטַבַּעַת זוּ, כְּדַת משֶׁה וְיִשְׂרָאֵל.

Haray aht m'kudeshet li b'taba'at zu k'dat Moshe v'Yisrael.
By this ring you are consecrated to me (as my wife)[19] *in accordance with the traditions of Moses and Israel.*

This formula, called the *haray aht*, contains thirty-two letters. In Hebrew, the number thirty-two is written with the letters *lamed* and *bet* (*vet*), which spell the word that means "heart"—*lev.* The groom thus gives his heart as he recites the words.

The custom of placing the ring on the bride's right index finger is said to be nearly a thousand years old. It may stem from an ancient belief that the index finger was directly connected by a special artery to the heart, so their hearts are joined.[20]

There are a number of explanations for the *halakhic* preference that the ring be placed on the index finger. Some suggest that this was where rings were once worn; others believe the custom simply made it easier to show witnesses that the bride had received the ring. By taking the ring on her most active finger the bride also demonstrates that she accepts it not as a gift but as a binding transaction. Today many couples prefer simply to place rings where they will be worn.

The Bride's Response. The bride is not legally required to say or do anything when she receives the ring. Some traditional Jews feel that the bride should not give the groom a ring or repeat the marriage formula because these actions then appear too much like an exchange and not a *kinyan,* which could jeopardize the *halakhic* validity of the marriage.

In most Jewish weddings today, however, the bride takes an active part in the ring ceremony. Typically, it is a virtual mirror of the groom's. She gives him a ring and recites the same formula, corrected for gender.

הֲרֵי אַתָּה מְקֻדָּשׁ לִי בְּטַבַּעַת זוּ כְּדָת מֹשֶׁה וְיִשְׂרָאֵל:

Haray ata m'kudash li b'taba'at zu k'dat Moshe v'Yisrael.
By this ring you are consecrated to me (as my husband) in accordance with the traditions of Moses and Israel.

There are a number of ways to acknowledge the bride's participation—particularly her assent, which is required by Jewish law, without making her actions appear to be an even exchange. In some instances the bride gives the groom a ring that is specified as a gift and therefore different from the object used for *kinyan.* Sometimes the bride will give the groom a ring later, during *yichud.*

Whether or not the bride gives the groom a ring, she may make some statement of acceptance. The absence of a specific formula for assent has been interpreted as permission for the bride to respond in her own way, using her own words and/or a biblical quotation. One of the most common responses is a quotation from Hosea: "I will betroth you to me forever. I will betroth you to me in righteousness, in justice, in love and in mercy. I will betroth you to me in faithfulness"; or "I am my beloved's and my beloved is mine. In accepting this ring, I consecrate myself to you as your wife in accordance with the traditions of Moses and Israel."

Vows. There are no wedding vows or "I do's" in the Jewish wedding liturgy. However, since this verbal exchange is such a powerful image in American culture, and since couples often feel a need to say "yes" in the course of the ceremony, many rabbis and couples add vows, to be spoken either just prior to or immediately following the ring ceremony.

Most rabbis avoid formulas identified with Christian wedding ceremonies, such as "To have and to hold, to honor and obey." Vows, or perhaps more accurately, "promises" or "intentions," can be very personal. Some brides and grooms write promises they read to each other. Or you can ask the rabbi to read a series of questions you've written—for example: "Do you, Len, promise to be patient with Rebecca, to laugh at her jokes and to comfort her tears, to live together as companions and lovers?" "Do you Dina, promise to be patient with Roger, to learn alongside him what it means to be human, what it means to love another person for a whole lifetime?"

Voices of Joy and Gladness

The ring ceremony completes betrothal/*kiddushin.* At this junction it has been customary, almost since the beginning of the combined betrothal-

and-nuptials wedding, to make a clear separation between the two ceremonies. Traditionally, this is done by having the rabbi read the *ketubah*
and hand it to the groom, who in turn gives it to the bride. The bride gives
the document to her parents or to an attendant for safekeeping.[21]

The custom of separating the two ceremonies with the *ketubah* reading is still in practice. The rabbi may read the Hebrew, or depending on
the text, the couple may even read it directly to each other as a way of ex-
changing "vows."

The bride can honor one of her attendants or guests by handing her or
him the *ketubah;* the attendant should be told in advance what to do with
the document once the ceremony is over. At some weddings, the *ketubah*
is passed from hand to hand; sometimes it is displayed on an easel during
the festivities later.

Generally this is when the rabbi makes a short speech. A rabbi who
knows you well may be able to express things about the two of you that
will be moving and important. If, however, you don't feel much of a connection with the rabbi, you can reasonably ask that she/he not feign
closeness and make his/her comments brief. If you'd like to add certain
things but are afraid you'll be too nervous to say or read them, you might
ask the rabbi to include your thoughts as part of the "sermon."

This natural break in the action is also a good time for personal additions to the ceremony. Special friends or family members may be invited
to read poems, prayers, and parables. See the section on "Wedding
Poems" beginning on page 219.

Although it is considered disrespectful to play music during the ceremony or *ketubah* reading, music can be integrated in the ceremony as a
sort of "backdrop" during these readings. Musically talented friends and
family members have presented couples with original songs and instru-
mental compositions to be sung or played under the *huppah* as special
wedding gifts.

This portion of the ceremony can even be extended to include all the
guests, who may read responsively or in unison from prayers in a wedding booklet or on sheets distributed before the ceremony begins. But re-

member: additional prayers, poems, or musical presentations should be kept short. Ten minutes of poetry or song can make the proceedings feel more like a concert than a wedding and overwhelm the liturgy, which is very brief.

Nuptials: The Seven Marriage Blessings

Nissuin, the second "half" of the wedding, consists of the *sheva b'rachot* (literally, seven blessings) and *yichud* (seclusion).

Set to ancient and evocative melodies, the blessings are the liturgical core of the wedding. Actually, it is perfectly legal to get married without these blessings, but reciting the *sheva b'rachot* is one of the customs that has taken on the force of law. It just doesn't *feel* like a Jewish wedding without them.

And in fact, the act of saying them transforms a wedding from an intimate act into a communal event. Legally, only two witnesses must be present to make the marriage valid, but you need ten Jews in order to recite these *b'rachot.* The presence of a minyan confirms the sense that every marriage builds a new "house" in Israel, forever changing the shape of the whole community.

There are many ways to "perform" the seven blessings. Usually, the rabbi or cantor will read or chant them all in Hebrew and English. But there is also a tradition of honoring special guests by asking them to read or chant a blessing either from their seats or under the *huppah.* In some communities it is the custom to ask married couples to do these honors. You can even ask everyone present to read the prayers in English, adding their voices to this chorus of blessing.

The Meaning of the Blessings. Given their importance, the order and even the relevance of some of these blessings can be confusing. For example, only two of them have anything to say about weddings, brides, and grooms, and these come at the very end. Yet read carefully and taken as a whole, the *sheva b'rachot* locate the couple under the *huppah* within the whole flow of Jewish history and theology.

The seven blessings sound many of the great themes of Judaism: creation, Eden, Zion, redemption, Jerusalem. Within this vast context, your wedding becomes the fulcrum of time. Your ceremony defines the center point between creation and redemption, between the first days and the end of days. All three of these "moments"—the beginning, your wedding, and the end—share the same wholeness, the same sweetness, and the unambiguous presence of God.

Your marriage represents answered prayers. Jewish mystics have long used the image of bridegroom and bride as a metaphor for redemption and wholeness. Since humankind left Eden, people have been in exile from that kind of shalom. And God has been in exile, too. The *Shechinah*, God's feminine self, is imagined as wandering the earth, cut off, and bereaved. On Shabbat, the day when we experience a taste of Eden and redemption, God and *Shechinah* are thought to be reunited as bride and bridegroom.

Judaism has no concept of individual redemption; we will each find Eden only when all human beings find Eden. The *sheva b'rachot* beneath your *huppah* provides the community with a glimpse into that redeemed, peace-filled, love-blessed place and time, which may be one of the reasons why weddings make us cry.

First Blessing

בָּרוּךְ אַתָּה יְיָ אֱלֹהֵינוּ מֶלֶךְ הָעוֹלָם, בּוֹרֵא פְּרִי הַגָּפֶן:

Blessed are you, Adonai our God, Ruler of the Universe who created the fruit of the vine.[22]

The Talmud mentions only six wedding blessings, but since the sixth century, Jews have made a universal practice of adding kiddush—the sanctification of God's name over wine—to round the number up to the much more mystically satisfying seven: the number of completion; the number of days it took God to create the universe; the number of perfection.

This second kiddush reiterates the sanctification and joy of the moment and serves as a liturgical "introduction" to the next three blessings, which celebrate creation. (The wine is not tasted until all seven *b'rachot* are recited.)

Second, Third, and Fourth Blessings

בָּרוּךְ אַתָּה יְיָ אֱלֹהֵינוּ מֶלֶךְ הָעוֹלָם, שֶׁהַכֹּל בָּרָא לִכְבוֹדוֹ:

Blessed are You, Adonai our God, Ruler of the Universe, who created everything for Your glory.

בָּרוּךְ אַתָּה יְיָ אֱלֹהֵינוּ מֶלֶךְ הָעוֹלָם, יוֹצֵר הָאָדָם:

Blessed are You, Adonai our God, Ruler of the Universe, shaper of humanity.

בָּרוּךְ אַתָּה יְיָ אֱלֹהֵינוּ מֶלֶךְ הָעוֹלָם, אֲשֶׁר יָצַר אֶת הָאָדָם בְּצַלְמוֹ, בְּצֶלֶם דְּמוּת תַּבְנִיתוֹ, וְהִתְקִין לוֹ מִמֶּנּוּ בִּנְיַן עֲדֵי עַד. בָּרוּךְ אַתָּה יְיָ, יוֹצֵר הָאָדָם:

Blessed are You, Adonai our God, Ruler of the Universe, who has shaped humanity in Your image, patterned after Your image and likeness, and enabled them to perpetuate this image out of their own being. Blessed are You, Adonai, shaper of humanity.

These three blessings praise God's creativity and generativity. The first, which blesses God for creating *hakol*, "all things," invokes the story in Genesis, where God makes the "heavens and the earth and everything in them." The creation of the universe and the creation of this marriage are linked, and in a sense, equated. The honor is enormous.

The next two blessings speak of the creation of Adam, or more generically, *adam,* humanity made of clay. Although they appear somewhat repetitive, they move from the general to the specific, and they include both the physical and the spiritual. First, we bless God for the sheer fact of *Adam's* creation—a miracle in itself. But then there is another blessing that suggests the special relationship between humankind and God; we are made in God's "image and likeness," not simply "God-like" but able to live in relationship to God.

This is a symbolic or mystical likeness, but the *b'racha* goes on to suggest the physical as well. Human beings have it in their power to "perpetuate this image out of their own being." Set in the context of the wedding ceremony, this becomes a benediction of love, marriage, and sexuality.

If creation is understood as an ongoing process, these three *b'rachot* are a challenge to fulfill our human potential for creativity and blessing, which God instilled in humanity on the sixth day of the first week, when God singled out the work of that day by pronouncing it "exceedingly good."

The blessings that celebrate the making of human beings are sometimes read by the couple's parents. This prayer is not recited at the time of a birth because babies are all and only potential; their humanity is still a question mark. By the time of a wedding, however, parents know whether their child has become a mensch deserving of this *b'racha;* thus reciting these blessings is a way of celebrating successful parenting.

Fifth Blessing

שׂושׂ תָּשִׂישׂ וְתָגֵל הָעֲקָרָה, בְּקִבּוּץ בָּנֶיהָ לְתוֹכָהּ
בְּשִׂמְחָה. בָּרוּךְ אַתָּה יְיָ, מְשַׂמֵּחַ צִיּוֹן בְּבָנֶיהָ׃

May the barren one exult and be glad as her children are joyfully gathered to her. Blessed are You, Adonai, who gladden Zion with her children.

This is probably the most confusing of the *sheva b'rachot,* the one given the freest translation and sometimes entirely rewritten. Of the many interpretations it has inspired, one of the more common equates Zion with Jerusalem, so the blessing fulfills the verse "Let my tongue stick to my palate if I do not place Jerusalem at the head of my joy." The holy city is mentioned before the rejoicing of bride and groom.

This blessing concretely extends the images of creation and continuity with talk of fertility, of a mother surrounded by children. The fifth blessing promises that God will reenact the miracle given to Sarah and Rachel—that barren women will be blessed with children—thus fulfilling the biblical promise of the continuation of the Jewish people.

According to Midrash, Zion is the center of the universe, the holiest place. Zion is where Adam was created, where the Temple stood, and where the word of God will issue forth at the end of days. When the messiah arrives—when time comes to an end—the souls of all the Jews who ever lived will find their way back to Zion. In a sense the fifth marriage blessing is a prayer for the redemptive unity of the end of days.

Alternative for the Fifth B'racha

> *Praised are you, Lord our God, who has given us a vision of the paradise we dream of creating with our lives and called it redemption. We praise you O Lord, who created the commitment of marriage as a foretaste of redemption.*
> —Rabbi Ramie Arian

Sixth and Seventh Blessings

שַׂמֵּחַ תְּשַׂמַּח רֵעִים הָאֲהוּבִים, כְּשַׂמֵּחֲךָ יְצִירְךָ בְּגַן עֵדֶן מִקֶּדֶם. בָּרוּךְ אַתָּה יְיָ, מְשַׂמֵּחַ חָתָן וְכַלָּה:

Grant great joy to these loving companions as You once gladdened your creations in the Garden of Eden. Blessed are You, Adonai, who gladden the bridegroom and the bride.

The bride and groom finally make an appearance! The comparison with the joy of Adam and Eve is a wish for perfect harmony; since the first two humans were created of the same dust, theirs was the most compatible marriage possible. The phrase "loving companions" is a particularly apt phrase for modern marriage, suggesting the importance of both passion and friendship in marriage.

The sixth and seventh blessings end with references to the couple under the *huppah*. However, in the sixth *b'racha* they are referred to as "bride *and* groom" and blessed separately. Their relationship as loving companions requires that each be able to stand alone even as they come together, bringing individual gifts to the marriage.

בָּרוּךְ אַתָּה יְיָ אֱלֹהֵינוּ מֶלֶךְ הָעוֹלָם, אֲשֶׁר בָּרָא שָׂשׂוֹן וְשִׂמְחָה, חָתָן וְכַלָּה, גִּילָה רִנָּה, דִּיצָה וְחֶדְוָה, אַהֲבָה וְאַחֲוָה, וְשָׁלוֹם וְרֵעוּת, מְהֵרָה יְיָ אֱלֹהֵינוּ יִשָּׁמַע בְּעָרֵי יְהוּדָה וּבְחוּצוֹת יְרוּשָׁלָיִם, קוֹל שָׂשׂוֹן, וְקוֹל שִׂמְחָה, קוֹל חָתָן וְקוֹל כַּלָּה, קוֹל מִצְהֲלוֹת חֲתָנִים מֵחֻפָּתָם, וּנְעָרִים מִמִּשְׁתֵּה נְגִינָתָם. בָּרוּךְ אַתָּה יְיָ, מְשַׂמֵּחַ חָתָן עִם הַכַּלָּה:

Blessed are You, Adonai our God, Ruler of the universe, who created joy and gladness, groom and bride, merriment, song, dance and delight, love and harmony, peace and companionship. Adonai our God, may there soon be heard in the cities of Judah and the streets of Jerusalem the voice of joy and the voice of gladness, the voice of the bridegroom and the voice of the bride, the rapturous voices of the wedded from their bridal chambers, and of young people feasting and singing. Blessed are You, Adonai, who gladden the bridegroom together with the bride.

In the last words of the final *b'racha* the bridegroom rejoices *with* the bride, united in joy, surrounded by ten degrees of joy and a chorus of jubilant voices. Here the ultimate joy of the end of days and the happiness of this wedding day become one and the same.

Given the economy of most rabbinic language, the ten synonyms for happiness in this blessing constitute an orgy of words, a mantra of the varieties of human joy. The enumeration of good feeling that ends the ceremony is an incitement for the guests to live up to their responsibility to entertain and rejoice with the bride and groom at the *s'eudah mitzvah*—the meal and celebration that follow.

Translations for the *Sheva B'rachot*

All translation is interpretation. The best translations straddle languages, conveying the meaning, rhythm, and style of the original while achieving integrity and beauty in their own right. Translation demands innumerable necessarily subjective decisions: How should "Adam" be translated? "Man" is a perfectly correct rendering of the Hebrew, but so is "humankind." Why translate "Adonai" at all? Strictly literal translations from Hebrew to English are virtually impossible due to differences in grammar; Hebrew nouns have gender, which requires changes in verb forms. And Hebrew and English deal with tenses very differently.

The following translations and interpretations of the *sheva b'rachot* include a variety of approaches to the text. All of them attempt to convey the spirit of the Hebrew—as the translators understand it.

Holy One of Blessing Your Presence fills creation, forming the fruit of the vine.

Holy One of Blessing Your Presence fills creation, as all creation reflects your splendor.

Holy One of Blessing Your Presence fills creation, giving life to each human being.

Holy One of Blessing Your Presence fills creation, You created man and woman in Your image, each reflecting the image of God for the other forever. Holy One of Blessing, You give life to every being.

How happy is she who thought herself childless and then finds that her children gather to rejoice within her. Holy One of Blessing, You make Zion happy with her children.

May these cherished friends rejoice in joy as You once rejoiced in Your creation of Gan Eden. Holy One of Blessing Your presence radiates joy for the bride and groom.

Holy One of Blessing Your Presence fills creation, You created joy and gladness, bridegroom and bride, delight, song, laughter and gaiety, love and harmony, peace and friendship. May all Israel soon ring with voices of gladness and joy, voices of bridegrooms and brides, voices raised in joyful wedding celebrations, voices lifted in festive singing. Holy One of Blessing Your Presence radiates for the bride and groom.

JOAN KAYE

Blessed are You, God, Source of the world, who creates the fruit of the vine.

Blessed are You, God, Light of life, who created everything for Your glory.

Blessed are You, God, Spirit of all things, who has created the human being.

Blessed are You, God, Foundation of every life, who fashioned humanity in Your likeness, and prepared for us a shape and form in Your image, from one generation to the next and for all eternity. Blessed are You, God, who has created human beings.

Zion will surely celebrate and exult in the coming together of her children. Blessed are You, God, who brings joy to Zion through her children.

Give pleasure to these beloved companions as You did to Your creation in the Garden of Eden so long ago. Blessed are You, God, who makes the hearts of this couple rejoice.

Blessed are You, God, Source of the universe, who has created each of these two people, their delight and their happiness, their rejoicing and singing, dancing and festivity, love and friendship, peace and pleasure. O God may the voices of this celebration be heard in the streets of our cities and the hills of our countryside. May the words of this couple go out with gladness from their wedding huppah, *and may the music of their friends and guests surround them. Blessed are You, God, who brings joy to the hearts of this couple.*

Janet Berkenfield

Blessed are you, God, who brings forth fruit from the vine.
Blessed are you, God, who shapes the universe.
Blessed are you, Holy One of Blessing, who fashions each person.

We bless you, God, for forming each person in your image. You have planted within us a vision of you and given us the means that we may flourish through time. Blessed are you, Creator of humanity.

May Israel, once bereft of her children, now delight as they gather together in joy. Blessed are you, God, who lets Zion rejoice with her children.

Let these loving friends taste of the bliss you gave to the first man and woman in the Garden of Eden in the days of old. Blessed are you, the Presence who dwells with bride and groom in delight.

Blessed are You, who lights the world with happiness and contentment, love and companionship, peace and friendship, bridegroom and bride. Let the mountains of Israel dance! Let the gates of Jerusalem ring with the sounds of joy, song, merriment, and delight—the voice of the groom and the voice of the bride, the happy shouts of their friends and companions. We bless you God, who brings bride and groom together to rejoice in each other.

Gilah Langner

Blessed are You, THE BOUNDLESS ONE our God, sovereign of all worlds, who creates the fruit of the vine.

Blessed are you, SOURCE OF LIFE our God, sovereign of all worlds, whose whole creation testifies to your glorious presence.

Blessed are You, KIND ONE our God, sovereign of all worlds, who fashions human beings.

Blessed are You, IMAGELESS our God, sovereign of all worlds, who has fashioned human beings in your image, patterning them in your likeness, and preparing them to share in the chain of life. Blessed are you, BELOVED ONE, who fashions human beings.

May Zion, the heart of our people, rejoice in the ingathering of all her children and all who join together in loving relationships. Blessed are you, THE WELCOMING ONE, who makes Zion rejoice with her children.

Make joyful these loving companions, O God—even as you once in the Garden of Eden made joyful your first couple. Blessed are you, DELIGHT, who makes joyful these loving companions.

Blessed are you, FAITHFUL ONE our God, sovereign of all worlds, who has created gladness and joy, loving partners, glee, song, mirth and exultation, harmony and love, and peace and companionship. Soon, O ETERNAL our God, may there be heard in the cities of Judah and in the streets of Jerusalem the voice of joy, the voice of gladness, the voices of loving partners from the huppah, *and from celebrations festive songs of young friends. Blessed are you, JOYFUL ONE, who brings loving companions together to rejoice in each other.*[23]

Rabbi's Manual of the Reconstructionist
Rabbinical Association

Blessed is the creation of the fruit of the vine.

Blessed is the creation which embodies glory.

Blessed is the creation of the human being.

Blessed is the design of the human being. Developing our wisdom we may become God-like. We are assembled from the very fabric of the universe and are composed of eternal element. Blessed be and Blessed is our creation.

Rejoice and be glad you who wandered homeless. In joy have you gathered with your sisters and your brothers. Blessed is the joy of our gathering.

Bestow happiness on these loving mates as would creatures feel in Eden's garden. Blessed be the joy of lovers.

Blessed is the creation of joy and celebration, lover and mate, gladness and jubilation, pleasure and delight, love and solidarity, friendship and peace. Soon may we hear in the streets of the city and the paths of the fields, the voice of joy, the voice of gladness, the voice of lover, the voice of mate, the triumphant voice of lovers from the canopy and the voice of youths from their feasts of song. Blessed Blessed Blessed is the joy of lovers, one with each other.

Adapted from the *sheva b'rachot* of
Linda Hirschhorn and David Cooper

The Seven Blessings

by Joel Rosenberg

Blessed is the One who plumps the grape
and makes the vine a sapphire necklace
curling through the humus of the vineyards
in the summer dew,

and blessed is the One whose world is weighty
like the crown of branches on the Tree of Life,

and blessed is the One who made the human being,
fashioned in the hands from humus
like a lump of clay,

and blessed is the One who gave the human,
humus-born, the light of breath and speech,
and made, from out of one, a two:
a lasting structure, formed and shaped
(who married all with joining words,
enjoining all to know about the nakedness
that may and may not be uncovered,
and about the promised ones whose touch
must be postponed, and gave forth unreservedly
companionship beneath the canopy, with words
across the cup of wine)!

Rejoice, rejoice, O devastated Lady!
Let Jerusalem rejoice! and let her womb
grow plump with children, gathered in
from wandering in other worlds,
like letters yearning to be speech,

and blessed is the One
who plants the fruit of joy
inside the citadel
atop her highest hill,

and dance and shout and sing, beloved friends,
  for in your laughter and your kisses
  is the blessed One, who gave us
  evanescent bliss in ancient days,
  inside the walled-in Garden
  watered endlessly by springs and mists,
  and blessed is that One who gives
  a taste of Eden to the bridegroom and the bride,

and blessed is the One who fashioned songs
  and ululations, dervish spinnings, ecstasies,
  prophetic tongues, and jokes and puns,
  and double meanings and new teachings,
  and renewal of the Teaching,
  and the passion between lovers,
  and affection between friends and kin,
  and blessed is the One who gave us strength
  and peace!

O quickly, quickly,
  Nameless One of ours, give Judah
  and the outskirts of Jerusalem
  the voice of weddings! Marry
  its inhabitants, and make us one
  with them, and make us One
  with You, and give us speech
  and poetry and pledges! Plump

the grape for us to bless,
and give us feasts and melodies,
and make us drunk with You,
O blessed One, who are
both Bridegroom and a Bride![24]

Finales

The Pronouncement. The *sheva b'rachot* conclude the marriage service. Some rabbis make their remarks at this point, but most simply end with the official pronouncement—"By the power vested in me by the state of . . . and according to the traditions of Moses and Israel . . ."—that the bride and groom are now husband and wife. Some add a benediction to conclude the ceremony, which may be the "priestly benediction" asking that God's presence and peace surround the couple and/or a very personal charge to the bride and groom.

The Broken Glass. It may be the best-known element of the Jewish wedding. It is entirely customary and essentially nonreligious. It is a very ancient practice encrusted with generations of interpretation. Few symbols can be given single, simple explanations, but the breaking of a glass at the end of the ceremony may be the most kaleidoscopic of all wedding symbols.

The broken glass is a joyous conclusion that encourages merriment at the *seudat mitzvah*—the meal of rejoicing—to follow. In modern times weddings have become rather solemn, but the shattering gives permission for levity to break out. There is an irony in this, since the breaking of a glass may have started as a way of toning down a particularly raucous wedding party.

The custom dates back to the writing of the Talmud.[25] "Mar bar Rabina made a marriage feast for his son. He observed that the rabbis present were very gay. So he seized an expensive goblet worth 400 zuzim and broke it before them. Thus he made them sober."[26] Rabina's point was, where there is rejoicing, there should be trembling.

By the Middle Ages, synagogue façades in Germany were inlaid with a special stone for the express purpose of smashing a glass at the end of weddings. However, the interpretation of the act had changed somewhat by the fourteenth century; it was seen as a reminder of the destruction of the Temple in Jerusalem.[27] Thus even at the height of personal joy, communal sadness is recalled.

This interpretation remains resonant, although it has been broadened to include all of the losses suffered by the Jewish people. The shattered glass is also seen as a reminder that although the wedding has provided a taste of redemption, the world is still in exile, broken and requiring our care. The glass is not only a reminder of sorrow but also an expression of hope for a future free from all violence.

A broken glass cannot be mended; likewise, marriage is irrevocable, divorce notwithstanding. It is a transforming experience that leaves individuals forever changed. It is a covenant between two people and also between a couple and God. In Judaism, covenants are "cut": at Sinai the tablets are broken, at a circumcision the flesh is marked. At a wedding the glass "cuts" the covenant.

The fragility of glass also suggests the frailty of human relationships. Even the strongest love is subject to disintegration. In this context, the glass is broken to "protect" the marriage with an implied prayer, "As this glass shatters, so may our marriage never break."

The making of loud noises is also an ageless method for frightening and appeasing demons, who, it was widely believed, were attracted to the beautiful and fortunate—people such as brides and grooms.

The breaking of a glass also has sexual connotations. It is a symbolic enactment of breaking the hymen, which explains why it was considered important that the groom "accomplish" the deed. Any failure was an embarrassing portent of impotence, and if the bride stepped on the glass, the groom's traditional role as *paterfamilias* was threatened. In a more general way, the breaking glass prefigures the intensity and release of sexual union, which is not only permitted to married couples but required of them.

Finally, the glass signals the end of the ceremony. The silence and hush of mythic time under the *huppah*—when the bride and groom stood as Adam and Eve, when redemption was almost tangible—ends with an explosion. People exhale, shout "Mazel tov!" clap their hands, embrace, talk, sing. Breaking the glass returns life to historical time where the world is still in *galut*—"exile"—although a little less broken as a result of the marriage.[28]

There are many opinions and customs regarding which glass is to be broken. According to some, one of the cups used for kiddush during the marriage should be shattered, with most opting for the goblet used for *kiddushin*/betrothal. After the *sheva b'rachot* the rabbi can empty the glass into a bowl, wrap it in a napkin, and hand it to the groom and/or bride to break. Somehow the irrevocability of cutting the marriage convenant becomes palpable when the couple crush a glass that helped sanctify their wedding.

It is also common for the couple to provide a third goblet, already wrapped and ready to be broken. This single wine glass can be a special gift from a friend or attendant, or it can be the occasion for a shopping excursion by the bride and groom. (Although a light bulb wrapped in a linen napkin is indistinguishable from a crystal goblet wrapped in a linen napkin, a sixty-watt bulb lacks something as a symbol.)

The glass should be wrapped to avoid injuries. Most people simply use a heavy cloth napkin, but some couples make or are given a special pouch for this purpose. Such a bag can be fashioned out of almost any material, in any design, and becomes an instant heirloom.

Although stepping on the glass was traditionally a groom's responsibility, some couples now share the act, equalizing the gesture and all its glorious implications.

The sound of breaking glass is greeted by shouts of "Mazel tov!" and a chorus of "Siman tov u mazel tov" as the couple depart. In some communities it is customary to lower the *huppah* over the couple for a moment of privacy immediately after the glass is broken.

Yichud. After they leave the *huppah,* bride and groom traditionally spend ten or fifteen minutes alone in *yichud*—seclusion. *Yichud* is an echo of ancient days when a groom would bring the bride to his tent to consummate the marriage. Although consummation has not immediately followed *huppah* for centuries, these moments of private time have remained as a symbolic consummation—a demonstration of the couple's right to privacy. (Physical consummation in the few minutes allowed for *yichud* would be entirely out of keeping with the Talmud's insistence that conjugal sex involve mutual consent, gentleness, patience, and joy.)

The word "consummation" means "bringing to completion" as well as sexual union, and *yichud* does provide a few moments for emotional consummation. It is a time to exhale, embrace, and let what has happened sink in. It is an important respite from the strain of being the center of attention for a whole day. It is an island of privacy and peace before the public celebration begins.

The *heder yichud,* the room in which the now married pair go to *yichud,* can be any private place. If the wedding has been held in a synagogue, the most common areas are the rabbi's study, the bride's room, or the library. In order to ensure the couple's privacy, "guards" may be posted outside the door to keep well-wishers away.

It is customary for the bride and groom to break their fast together during *yichud,* sharing their first meal as husband and wife. There are various customs about what special foods should be eaten. Among Ashkenazim it is "golden soup"—chicken soup, a food that suggests prosperity and builds strength. This may be served in a beautiful tureen, sometimes a special gift from a family member or close friend. In some Sephardic communities the couple is served a meal of doves, symbolic of marital peace.

If neither chicken soup nor dove appeals to you, ask a friend to provide a plate piled with your favorite foods: chocolate, taco chips, bread and butter, whatever. Instruct the caterer to prepare a tray of hors d'oeuvres, which you might otherwise not taste. It is traditional for the bride and groom to feed each other during *yichud,* a token that they will sustain each other throughout their marriage. Since most wedding celebrations include wine or champagne, and most couples don't have the time or the inclination to eat much during the meal, it's a good idea to eat something during *yichud.*

Yichud makes it impossible to assemble a receiving line immediately following the ceremony. It is, however, a way of keeping the emphasis where it is supposed to be in a Jewish wedding—on the joy of the bride and groom, not on the expectations of the guests. After *yichud* the bride and groom are announced for the first time as husband and wife. They may be greeted with a toast, with a shower of candy or rice, with singing and dancing.

BLESSINGS FOR THE SIMCHA

BEFORE THE MEAL

It is customary to begin the meal after the ceremony with a blessing over a wedding challah—an especially large, elaborately braided loaf of the egg-rich bread that is a regular feature of the Sabbath table as well. There are a number of simple ways to make this brief *b'racha* into a special moment in the proceedings.

The bride and groom can together lead the blessing, and then bring a piece of the challah to each table, which gives them a chance to greet everyone personally. Or the *hamotzi* can be recited by parents of the bride and groom or any other honored guests.

בָּרוּךְ אַתָּה יְיָ אֱלֹהֵינוּ מֶלֶךְ הָעוֹלָם הַמּוֹצִיא לֶחֶם מִן הָאָרֶץ:

Baruch ata Adonai, Eloheynu Melech Ha-olam, hamotzi lechem min ha-aretz.

Praised are you Adonai, Ruler of the universe, who brings bread from the earth.

Sheva Shevahot. According to tradition, only men are counted in the minyan, only men may serve as witnesses, only men chant the *sheva b'rachot,* both under the *huppah* and following the wedding feast. Orthodox women may not be comfortable breaking with these traditions; however, the need to honor and include female relatives and friends at wedding celebrations has prompted the creation of a new ritual form: *sheva shevahot*—seven praises.[29]

Drawing on the biblical examples of Miriam, who gathered the women of Israel to celebrate the Exodus from Egypt, and Devorah, who judged and claimed victories in poems and songs, the seven praises are a way of giving voice to women's joy and gladness. Paralleling the *sheva b'rachot* that will follow the meal, *sheva shevahot* are recited before the meal. The seven praises can mirror the themes of the *sheva b'rachot,* or they may concentrate on the bride and groom, honoring their names, their abilities, their plans. Psalms and poems, lines from Song of Songs, and references to biblical foremothers are common resources: "And Miriam the prophetess, the sister of Aaron, took the timbrel in her hand; and all the women went out after her with timbrels and with dances" (Exodus 15:20). *Shehehiyanu,* the familiar and powerful prayer of thanksgiving for new blessings, is often used as the seventh praise.

Concluding the Festivities

Weddings tend to fizzle to their conclusions; guests trickle out the door, and the bride and groom wonder when it's permissible for them to leave. But the traditional way to end a *s'eudat mitzvah* is by chanting *birkat hamazon,* the blessings after the meal, which closes the day with spirit, dignity, and finality.

The prayer is sung by everyone present, responsively and in unison. If guests are familiar with the words and melodies of *birkat hamazon,* this can be a powerful affirmation of love and community. If, however, you and/or many of your guests are unfamiliar with the Hebrew prayers, they can be chanted or read in English, or even adapted and amended.

Booklets called *benchers* containing the *birkat hamazon* are distributed. *Benchen* is Yiddish for praying, particularly prayers after eating. Wedding *benchers* often bear the bride and groom's names and the date, and sometimes the *birkat hamazon* is included in the wedding booklet. (See page 199.) Different kinds of *benchers* can be purchased at Jewish book stores; some are entirely in Hebrew, some provide the English translation, and many include traditional songs. Or you can create a *bencher,* with a translation and songs of your own choosing. The *birkat hamazon* is found in most *siddurim* (daily prayer books). One translation appears at the end of this section.

When it is time to conclude, a designated leader invites the guests to open their *benchers* for *birkat hamazon.* People usually return to their tables for *benching;* but sometimes a small table at which the bride and groom are seated will be set up in the middle of the dance floor, and everyone gathers around them for the final prayers of the day.

After *birkat hamazon* at weddings, the seven marriage blessings may be repeated, except that this time the blessing over wine is read last. The blessings are often distributed among special people who did not participate under the *huppah.* (Such an honor should never come as a surprise; inform the people you select well in advance.) Each *b'racha* can be shared between a couple or a pair of friends, one of whom chants the Hebrew while the other reads an English translation.

And finally, it is traditional to end with the ceremony of the cups. A full goblet of wine is held aloft by a leader of the *benching* during *birkat hamazon.* A second goblet is poured before the *sheva b'rachot* are sung again. With the words "bo-rey p'ree ha-gaffen," wine from both cups is mixed in a third goblet, from which the bride and groom drink. This third cup may then be shared with the couple's parents and/or passed around the room.

This "cup of blessing" represents the combined joy of bride and groom, the completion of both betrothal and nuptials, the establishment of a new entity—a marriage in which all elements are shared. It is a pouring of two lives into one, a hope for future generations, for the unification of all apparent opposites.

The kiddush cups used under the *huppah* are usually incorporated into this ceremony, and some couples purchase a third, large goblet for mixing the wine together. This goblet can become a family treasure, used for Elijah's cup at Passover seders. It can also be the cup used for Jewish ceremonies to welcome the birth of a child.

Benching for Beginners. *Birkat hamazon* is not a spectator sport. Even if a majority of guests are unfamiliar with Hebrew, it can be orchestrated so that everyone can participate. Hebrew can be integrated in a number of ways into *benching* that is mostly English. One person can lead the Hebrew-speaking guests in the chanting while another person leads the rest of the company through the same passage in English, or sections can be alternated in Hebrew and English.

If you want to encourage guests to offer personal blessings during the *harachamon* (petitionary prayers that begin with the word *harachamon*) portion of the *benching,* it's a good idea to tell at least some of your guests in advance. Then, when the leaders ask for prayers from the company, there can be a "spontaneous" outpouring of good wishes. Or every table might be asked to compose a collective wish on a particular theme: health, home, livelihood, prosperity, peace, children, and so on. A note-card with a specific "assignment" for each table will facilitate this.

Birkat Hamazon—Blessings after the Meal

The blessings consist of four benedictions on different themes: thanking God who provides food; blessing the land that produces it; expressing hope for the rebuilding of Zion; and attesting to God's goodness and love. These are followed by a series of petitions generally called the *harachamons,* each of which begins with that word, which means "O Merciful One." (The *harachamons* are sometimes changed to suit the occasion.) Verses from Psalms follow, and the *birkat hamazon* ends with a prayer for peace. On joyful occasions the *birkat hamazon* is preceded by Psalm 126.

PSALM 126: A Reaching-Up Song[30]

When God returned us
To Zion from exile,
We thought we were dreaming.
Then our mouths filled with laughter
And cheers were on our tongue.
The other nations saw and said,
"The Lord has done great things for them."
The Lord has done great things for us,
And we were very glad.
Return us again to freedom, Adonai,
Like streams, long dry, to the Negev returning.
Those who sow in tears
Will reap in joy.
The farmer wants to weep
When he buries the precious seed,
But singing he comes back
With his arms filled with grain.

THE INVITATION AND CONSENT

LEADER: Friends! Let us give thanks!

COMPANY: May God's name be praised now and forever!

LEADER: With your consent, then, let us praise God from whose abundance we have eaten.

COMPANY: Praise God from whose abundance we have eaten and by whose goodness we live.

ALL: Praise God, Praise God!

BLESSING FOR FOOD: *Birkat Hazan*

Holy One of Blessing, Your Presence fills creation,
You nourish the world with goodness
and sustain it with grace, loving kindness and mercy.
You provide food for every living thing because
You are merciful. Because of Your great goodness,
the earth yields its fruit. For Your sake
we pray that we shall always have enough to eat,
for You sustain and strengthen all that lives and
provide food for the life that You created.
Holy One of Blessing, You nourish all that lives.

BLESSING FOR THE LAND: *Birkat Haaretz*

We thank You, God, for the good land that you gave
to our parents as a heritage; for liberating us from
the soft slavery of Egypt; for the Covenant You sealed
in our flesh; for the Torah that You teach us; for the
laws that You reveal to us; for the life that
You have given us and for the food which nourishes
and strengthens us each day; even as it does right now.
We thank You, God, for all Your gifts
and praise You, as all who live must praise You each
   day;
for You teach us in your Torah: "When you have
   eaten
your fill, you shall praise God for the
good land that God has given you."
Holy One of Blessing,
we thank You for the land and its fruit.

BLESSING FOR JERUSALEM: *Birkat Yerushalayim*

Oh God, have compassion on Israel, Your people;
on Jerusalem, Your city; on Zion, the home of Your
glory;
on the royal house of David, Your anointed, and
upon the great and holy Temple that was called
by Your name. Dear God, tend us, nourish us, sustain
us
and support us; and, dear God, relieve us soon from
all of our troubles. O God, let us never depend upon
the charity of our fellows, but let us depend on
Your generous help alone, so that we may never be put
to shame.
And build Jerusalem, the holy city, soon, in our day!
Holy One of
Blessing, Your compassion builds Jerusalem.

THE BLESSING OF GOODNESS: *Birkat Hatov V'hametiv*

Holy One of Blessing, Your Presence fills creation,
You are our Redeemer, our Maker, our Holy One,
the Holy One of Jacob. You are the Shepherd of Israel,
the good Sovereign, who does good for all. As You do
good each day, so, we pray, do good things for us.
As You provide for us each day, so, we pray, treat us
with loving kindness and compassion, relieve us from
our troubles and grant us prosperity and redemption,
consolation, sustenance and mercy: a good and peaceful
life.
Never withhold Your goodness from us.

THE HARACHAMON PETITIONS

May the Merciful One rule over us now and forever!
O Merciful One, You are praised in the heavens as
You are
praised on earth.
O Merciful One, You will be praised by every generation
and You will be honored among us forever.
May the Merciful One deliver us from oppression and give
us freedom.
May the Merciful One bless this house and all who have
shared our meal.
May the Merciful One send Elijah the prophet,
may he be remembered for good, to bring us the good news of
redemption and consolation.
May the Merciful One bless us and all who are dear to us
with the perfect blessing that God bestowed on our parents,
Abraham and Sarah, Isaac and Rebecca, and Jacob, Leah
and Rachel.
May we be worthy of peace, O God, and the blessings of
justice from the God of our salvation and may we find
grace and understanding in the sight of God and all
peoples.

Additional blessings for Rosh Hodesh may be included at this point—for example: "May the Merciful One renew for us this month His goodness and blessing."

Petitionary prayers of all kinds are commonly added here. In the spirit of the day, the leader of the *benching* might add special personal *harachamons* as well—for example:

May the Merciful One bless Jess and David with shalom in their hearts and under their roof.

May the Merciful One bless the parents of Jess and the parents of David with many more years of joy and *naches* from their children.

May the Merciful One bless Jess and David with a sense of humor in times of minor difficulties and with patience in times of distress.

May the Merciful One bless this company, and allow us all to gather soon and often for such joyous occasions.

The *birkat hamazon* then continues:

> *May Merciful God find us worthy of*
> *the Messiah and of life in the world to come.*
> *You are a tower of strength to Your king*
> *and are compassionate to Your anointed, David,*
> *and his descendants now and forever.*
> *May God, who makes peace on high,*
> *bring peace to us and to all Israel.*

Many people choose to end the *birkat hamazon* here, with this prayer for peace. The last two lines are set to a lively melody familiar to many Jews. The transliteration of these lines can encourage a participatory and upbeat conclusion to the *benching:*

> *Oseh shalom bimromav, hu ya-seh shalom*
> *Alienu v'al kol Yisroel v'rimeru, Omein.*

But a complete rendering of the *birkat hamazon* continues with the following, which consists of a collection of verses from Psalms:

Fear God, you holy ones,
for those who fear God will feel no want.
Even the strong may lack and hunger
but those who seek God will lack for nothing that is good.
Let us thank God, for God is good.
Your compassion endures forever. You open Your hand
and satisfy every living thing with favor.
You who trust God are blessed, for God will protect you.
I have been young and now I am old,
yet never have I seen the righteous abandon those who lack
    bread.
God will give strength to God's people
God will bless the people with peace.

PART FOUR

CREATING A JEWISH HOME

LIVING AS BRIDE AND GROOM

When a man takes a new wife, he shall be deferred from military duty, he shall not be charged with any business. He shall be free for his house one year and shall cheer his wife, whom he has taken. —Deuteronomy 24:5

Sheva B'rachot: A Week for Celebration. For many generations brides and grooms spent their first week of married life surrounded by their communities, entertained and fed for a full week at special, festive meals also called *sheva b'rachot*. The seven days of community participation following a wedding correspond to the seven days after a death. Both are perceived as periods of transition when people are vulnerable and in need of community protection against what were once called evil spirits, but which could be given other names. Any major life change provokes anxiety. After a death one needs protection against despair. When a bride and groom were barely acquaintances before their wedding, a couple needed support through their initial shyness and awkwardness. Like *shiva*, the seven days of mourning, *sheva b'rachot* lets a couple know they are not alone.

A *minyan*—a gathering of ten observant Jews—assembled every evening for a week and, after eating, repeated *birkat hamazon*. If at least one *panim chadashot*—"new face"—was present, the seven marriage blessings were added at the end of those blessings. These parties often lasted late into the night and eventually included nearly everyone in the community.

Although very traditional couples still postpone their wedding trips for a week in order to celebrate with family and friends, the getaway honeymoon has displaced the custom of *sheva b'rachot* for most of the Jewish community.

The First Year. Since biblical times the special status of "bride and groom" has lasted for a full year—a year full of changes and congratulations. It is a year for bonding and growth, sharing and learning. The year-long public recognition of the special status of brides and grooms is a way for the community to savor their joy and share their happiness.

The designations "husband" and "wife" really apply only after that first year, when a home is established and, as the Torah suggests, the couple have consummated many aspects of their relationship. A year's seasons and a full cycle of Jewish holidays are shared as bride and groom: a first springtime and Pesach, a first autumn and Yom Kippur.

A Jewish Home

When the world was created,
God made everything a little bit incomplete.
Rather than making bread grow out of the earth,
God made wheat grow so that we might bake it into bread.
Rather than making the earth of bricks,
God made it of clay
so that we might bake the clay into bricks. Why?
So that we might become partners
in completing the work of creation.[1]

According to the Zohar, the central book of Jewish mysticism, God creates new worlds constantly by causing marriages to take place. The venue of each of these new worlds is a home, which is symbolically established by a *huppah*. But a *huppah* is an outline that needs to be filled, shaped, and named by the people who have chosen to inhabit it, "its few lines a sketch for what might be."[2]

For traditional Jews, *halakhah* provides a fairly straightforward description of the Jewish home: it has a kosher kitchen, its doorposts are marked with mezuzahs, Shabbat and the holidays are celebrated according to Jewish law, sexual relations between husband and wife are regulated by the laws of *taharat hamishpachah*—the laws of family purity.

For liberal Jews, the definition of a Jewish home is more flexible and problematic. Is it a Jewish home if a non-Jew marries a Jew? Is it a Jewish home if Shabbat candles are never lit, but the Jews who live there volunteer unselfishly on behalf of the local Jewish federation. Is it a Jewish home if great amounts of money are given to the Jewish community while bacon fries in the kitchen? Is it a Jewish home if no one ever gives the question a thought?

One *ketubah* describes the commitment to establishing a Jewish home as a pledge to be "open to the spiritual potential in all life wherein the flow of the seasons and the passages of life are celebrated through the symbols of our Jewish heritage. A home filled with reverence for learning, loving, and generosity. A home wherein ancient melody, candles and wine sanctify the table. A home joined ever more closely to the community of Israel."[3]

Some of the elements that constitute a Jewish home include: the presence of ritual items (a mezuzah at the door, Shabbat candlesticks, a kiddush cup, and so on); observance of Shabbat and the holidays; observance of *kashrut;* Jewish books and a reverence for learning; *tsedakah* —charity—given within the Jewish community; *hachnasat orchim*— hospitality; affiliation with a synagogue and other Jewish organizations. These commitments and others are generally addressed by rabbis during premarital meetings, not as a laundry list of do's and don'ts but as a prospectus for a lifelong exploration of Jewishness. A Jewish home is not a static entity; it changes.

A wedding marks a Jewish beginning, a time for experimenting with the varied forms and flavors of Jewishness. Each person begins with his or her own notions about observance and affiliation, which probably means that you, as a couple, will need to search out a path you can share.

The Jewish home is sometimes called a *mikdash ma'at*—a little sanctuary. It is a powerful image. A sanctuary feels different from a place of business. Sanctuaries elicit special moods and emotions and invite a quality of self-consciousness found in few other man-made structures. The threshold of a *mikdash,* marked by a mezuzah, creates a separation that defies the modern notion that all places are essentially the same, that space is empty of meaning.

Sanctuaries invite people to enter for unquantifiable encounters. Sanctuaries affirm that community is as necessary as bread. A sanctuary is a place of rest, safety, and asylum. The place that, by definition, will shelter the dispossessed, feed the hungry, and allow the possibility that *this* wandering beggar may be the prophet Elijah, who will never announce redemption if he is mistreated. Sanctuaries are never closed to people who come honestly, openly, seeking, which is why the sanctuary's money is given freely where it is needed.

The *mikdash* is a place of books but it is not a hushed library. Discussion, debate, even loud disagreements are welcome here.

Sanctuaries are visibly different from other places. They are marked off by symbols. They are filled with voices, sometimes reading in unison and sometimes raised in passionate debate. There is music in the sanctuary and occasionally the deep, living silence of a garden.

No synagogue sanctuary is perpetually filled with all the meaning and being it is called to. No home is every fully or finally a sanctuary. There are only degrees of intention.

Tay-Sachs and Allied Diseases

Due to the prevalence of Tay-Sachs and other rare hereditary diseases among Jews of Eastern European descent (Ashkenazic), many rabbis require couples to undergo genetic testing as part of their premarital counseling sessions.

Tay-Sachs disease, an inherited disorder of the central nervous system, is one hundred times more common in Jewish children than in non-Jewish children. The cause of Tay-Sachs disease is the absence of a vital enzyme called hexosaminidase A (Hex A), which the body uses to break down fatty substances (lipids) in the brain. Without the Hex A enzyme, lipids accumulate and eventually destroy brain function. By the age of about six months, a baby with Tay-Sachs disease loses physical skills, sight, and the ability to eat or smile. There is no known cure for the disease, and death usually occurs by five years of age.

Carriers of the Tay-Sachs gene do not have the disease themselves, but if two carriers conceive a child, there is a one-in-four chance that a pregnancy will result in an afflicted baby. A simple blood test determines whether an adult is a carrier. Some couples who find out that both partners carry the Tay-Sachs gene choose to adopt rather than try to conceive. Others decide to use artificial insemination with sperm from someone who does not carry the gene. Still others conceive and use prenatal testing as a second line of prevention.

Amniocentesis, removal of a small quantity of fluid from the uterus early in the second trimester of pregnancy, can determine whether the fetus has Tay-Sachs. If the child is found to have the disease, a couple may choose to terminate the pregnancy.

Judaism takes a nuanced approach to the practice of abortion. Even the most conservative interpretation of Jewish law allows abortion to save the life of the mother, and many Jewish authorities permit abortion if the birth would cause the mother mental anguish and suffering. In cases where there is evidence of severe prenatal defects or genetic disease, Jewish law sanctions abortion not from the perspective of the child, but in order to spare the mother's pain at the inevitable loss of the child.

It is beyond the scope of this book to treat these issues in depth, but given the emotional and ethical impact that can follow genetic testing, it can be enormously helpful to talk with a rabbi as well as a physician. In addition to providing counseling, your rabbi may be able to refer you to thoughtful genetic counselors as well as specialists and support groups.

For more information about Tay-Sachs and the other rare genetic lipid storage diseases that affect Jews, contact: The National Tay-Sachs and Allied Diseases Association, 2001 Beacon Street, Suite 204, Brighton, MA 02135, 800-906-8723, www.ntsad.org.

Divorce

According to the Talmud, when a marriage is dissolved, "even the altar sheds tears."[4] Divorce has, however, been a fact of Jewish life since the Torah. In its attempt to sanctify all aspects of human experience, Jewish law is as concerned with the dissolution of marriage as with its creation.

A traditional Jewish divorce involves the writing of a formal document called a *get,* which is commissioned by the husband, delivered to the wife, and acknowledged by a *bet din,* a rabbinical court. While there are a few cases in which a wife can obtain a *get* or compel her husband to give her one, traditional Jewish divorce, like marriage, is essentially a male prerogative that requires the man to take action. A marriage that has not been dissolved "according to the traditions of Moses and Israel" is considered binding on the woman.

A woman who hasn't obtained a *get*—even if she has been granted a civil divorce—may not remarry as a Jew. She is called *agunah*—literally, "one who is chained." If she remarries—under any religious or secular authority—her children will be illegitimate (*mamzerim*) and, according to Jewish law, may never marry Jews. (Again, this is not the case for husbands, whose subsequent children, born of Jewish wives, are legitimate.)

All Orthodox and many Conservative rabbis will not officiate at a second marriage without first having ascertained that the divorced parties have obtained a *get*.

A traditional *get*, like a traditional *ketubah*, is written in Aramaic. It must be executed by a *sofer*, a professional scribe, and it must be absolutely clear in meaning.

Traditional *Get*

On the ___ day of the week, the ___ day of the month of _____ in the year ___ from the creation of the world according to the calendar reckoning we are accustomed to count here, in the city _____ which is located on the river _____ and _____, I do willingly consent, being under no restraint, to release, to set free, and put you aside, my wife _____ daughter of _____ who are today in the city of _____, which is located on the river _____ and _____, who has been my wife. Thus do I set free, release you and put you aside, in order that you may have permission and the authority over yourself to go and marry any man you may desire. No person may hinder you from this day onward, and you are permitted to every man. This shall be for you a bill of dismissal from me, a letter of release, and a document of freedom, in accordance with the laws of Moses and Israel.

Signed by two witnesses:

Once the wife (or her proxy) has accepted the *get*, she gives it to a *bet din*, which in turn gives her a document stating that she is divorced according to Jewish law and free to remarry. The *get* is then symbolically torn, showing that the covenant is nullified.

There is an organized effort among Modern Orthodox women and rabbis—in North America, Israel, and around the world—to expedite the writing of *gittim* (the plural of *get*). Many Orthodox and Conservative rabbis also encourage a prenuptial agreement that spells out a promise to seek a *get* in the event of divorce.[5] (See Prenuptial agreement on page 236.)

Non-Orthodox American Jews who contemplate settling in Israel sometimes seek an Orthodox *get*. In Israel, where Orthodox rabbinical courts are the civil authority for marriage and divorce law, the children of a woman considered *agunah* sometimes have difficulty getting licenses to marry other Jews. (Israeli military men commonly have a *get* written in advance in case they should ever be "missing in action" for a long period of time.)

Non-Orthodox Responses

In the nineteenth century the Reform movement decided that civil divorce was fully valid and that no special Jewish recognition of the dissolution of a marriage was necessary. This decision was based largely upon the fact that the *get* ran counter to Reform's principle of complete equality in religious status for men and women. To this day, the vast majority of Reform and Reconstructionist rabbis perform a second marriage without a *get*.

No more than 10 percent of divorced Jews seek a *get*.[6] Since somewhere between one-third and one-half of all Jewish marriages end in divorce, most American Jews clearly consider civil divorce sufficient and valid. However, there is new interest in providing Jewish closure to marriages that end in divorce.

The Conservative movement, which considers itself bound by the process of *halakhah* (Jewish law), officially prohibits its rabbis from performing ceremonies if either the bride or groom was previously divorced without a *get*. To achieve this goal, many Conservative *ketubot* contain a clause stating that, after a civil divorce, both members of the couple agree to appear before a *bet din* for the purposes of ending their union according to Jewish law. (See the description of the Lieberman clause, described in the chapter on the *ketubah,* and the documents in the appendix on Betrothal/ *Tenaim.*)

Regardless of affiliation, many people find meaning and healing in a Jewish rite that formally acknowledges the end of a relationship that began under Jewish auspices. Non-Orthodox divorce rituals and documents are generally reciprocal rather than unilateral, with both partners symbolically granting each other permission to remarry and also affirming a new start for themselves.

In the *get* below, two copies are written; one is given by the woman to the man, one by the man to the woman. The rabbi retains a third copy for his or her files. The text appears side by side in Hebrew and English.

Liberal *Get*

On the _____ day of the week, the _____ day of the month of _____ five thousand seven hundred _____ years since the creation of the world as we reckon here in _____ located near _____ daughter/son of _____ who resides in _____ said to _____ son/daughter of _____ I, of my own free will, grant you this bill of divorce. I hereby release you from the contract which established our marriage. From today onward, you are not my husband/wife and I am not your wife/husband. You belong to yourself and are free to marry again.

Signed by the woman, the man, two witnesses, and rabbi.[7]

The following passage may be added:

With this *Get,* I _____, free you, _____, from all vows and commitments of marriage made under Jewish tradition.

I turn to the source of life and love:

Let me not pray to be sheltered from dangers, but to be fearless in facing them.

Let me not beg for the stifling of my pain, but for the heart to conquer it.

Let me not crave in anxious fear to be saved, but hope for the patience to win my freedom.

Give me the strength to make my love fruitful in service.

Let hurt disappear and anger dissipate, and may I find in my freedom the power to face all my tomorrows.[8]

This kind of get might be executed in a rabbi's study or synagogue sanctuary. If only one spouse is present for the ceremony, the document may be read and later delivered to the other. If both the man and woman are present, each brings a friend to act as witness and support. The ceremony can consist of just a few words from the rabbi and the reading of the divorce documents. The copy that remains on file with the rabbi is symbolically cut or ripped, to physically enact the dissolution of the marriage covenant. The rabbi may pronounce the man and woman free to begin their new lives and marry whom they choose. While any formal acknowledgment of divorce is invariably painful, ceremonies such as these often provide a welcome sense of resolution.[9]

For everything there is a season
and a time for every purpose under heaven:
A time to be born and a time to die,
a time to plant and a time to uproot . . .
a time for tearing down and a time for building up
a time for weeping and a time for laughing . . .
a time for embracing and a time to refrain from embracing.

APPENDICES

Wedding Poems

The First Wedding in the World

By Joel Rosenberg

I

The eighth day was the wedding.
He awoke amid a dewy moss,
and saw two swans gliding
between the cattails. It was dawn.

His side felt sore. He felt
a yearning where before
he'd felt protected, like a dream
had stolen out of reach.

It still was early,
and the moon still gleamed,
and crickets still posed
questions to their answering chorus.

Two large lions sat nearby,
amid the mist,
placidly gazing at the tiny rabbits
nibbling lettuce in their grassy niches.

II

The man had never seen an angel.
He thought it strange
that rainbow-colored fire
took on human image.

When he met Michael
and Gabriel, who told him
they were witnesses,
he thought their garments

were cascades of golden leaves,
their eyes a burning agate,
and their wings
a wreath of northern lights.

He called some names,
and beast and fowl
perked up their ears,
and forest noises filled the air.

III

God had the woman
waiting for him near the meadow,
standing on a shell,
her hair down to her knees.

She thought it all so strange,
this garden, jabbering animals,
this stranger standing dumbfounded
and stuttering out her name in joy.

She'd never seen a wedding canopy.
The golden gauze
was spun by angels
in the middle of the night.

She thought herself
a thousand years of age,
though looking like a girl of twenty,
all the sad, expensive wisdom

of society about to waken
in her bones, the secrets
of the wind and stars,
the human arts

of strife and cultivation,
tincture of the eyelids,
epic meters, and, as well,
concealments and apologies.

She smiled at the young man's
innocence, while, lovingly,
and for forever, she held out
her hand to him.

IV

The two of them,
with honeybees weaving among
the wreaths of flowers
at their brows,

the two of them,
with hope for clothes,
and no disqualifying memories,
and nothing that was not

within them from the start,
the two of them joined hands
and stood before the shimmering light
to make their vows.[1]

A Shepherd's Song in Midian

BY JOEL ROSENBERG

I betroth you to me for an aeon,
I betroth you by the halo of the moon,
I bind to me, with you,
as I would bind a sign upon my hand,
the cricket antistrophes,
the rainbow and the quail.

I bind us by the fire on this mountain,
by the crackling thunder,
by the dancing alphabet above these rocks,
the sparking sage and bramble,
and the fleeing panther,
and the hind, poised, pausing
in her tracks.

Stand by me
in this yawning niche,
so recessed, like our vision,
yielding only outlines
of the past,

and I will place my shelter over you,
and, by the kernel of the pomegranate,
by the orange, and by the coriander,
by the henna of the lion's mane,
and by the oxen of the wood,
and by the learning of the elders,
and the merits of our mothers
Hannah, Sarah and Hagar,
and by the pain of Egypt,
and the steam of Goshen,
by the murmuring amid the tribes,
and by the shade of the tamar,

we'll tie aground the sky,
and open up the fountains in the granite,
and we'll split the seas like wineskins,
and we'll throw down history like a carpet
paved with snow and sapphire stones,
seen from afar.

And I will be a laborer for you,
and make the angels honor you,
and feed you words of manna,
and support you with a mighty hand.
And if I speak in stammers on your heart,
I'll speak to you with winning words,
and tell you: "Live, and flourish
like a sprouting of the field,"
and you shall know me, not
by names of mastery,
but you shall know me as your twin.

And I will bear you up on eagle's wings,
and I will guide you to a land
with skins of mists and dews,
her earth a garment for the body
of the dead,
and read to you the text of memory,
and tell you what was never said.

And I betroth you to me here,
correctly, even-temperedly,
but caring, and with tenderness.
My nurturing you'll know,
and I will be what I will be,
and you will be what you will be.
And who on earth has ever heard
about a union such as ours,
and who on earth has ever said
what we have said?[2]

The Mystery of Union

BY JOEL ROSENBERG

As they, above, unite in one,
becoming One amid the mystery
of union, so, here below,

by call of ptarmigan and tern,
through summer cirrus feathers,
clove and fern, by symmetry

of witness, by the hand of scribe,
and ripening of time, we find
a place as one.

The hind
has panted for the stream.
The binding of the hand

has spelled the ancient themes
upon the heart. A gleam
of angels dances at the edges

of our words, while tablets
of our covenant
are hewn. A team of doves,

released like mist, the skirring
of their wings inscribe
a life's reunion with itself,

as you and I remember
how we stood together even then:
cicada, wind and thunder

growing dumb, the seaswells
hushed, Sambatyon
in pause. No lion roared,
no cattle lowed,
no horses neighed,
no peacocks crowed—

for one small instant
silence reigned, throughout
even the temples and the markets

of the Nile, while, slowly,
hardly louder than an aleph,
came the words: "I am"
and: "I am yours." [3]

Renewal of the Moon

BY JOEL ROSENBERG

The sun and moon, born
on the fourth day of Creation,
quarreled over who should have
more light.

And the Creator
made the moon's light a reflection
of the sun's, and made it ebb
and grow.

God said
to them: "To keep you
from your quarreling,
I'll give you both a task.
Together, you must share
one light, and pass it
back and forth. By you
the people of the world
will set their clocks
and calendars. Therefore,
be one: Cooperate and grow!"

And in the Garden,
the Creator told the man & woman:
"You shall have one light,
as well, and pass it
back and forth, so that it seems
now one of you and now the other
has more strength. But inwardly,
you are the same. And since
all peoples of the earth will come
from you, you must cooperate.
And you shall be a tree
of nations—light of knowledge,
tree of life!"

And the Creator
made a nation like the moon,
and called it "Israel," telling her:
"Be many, and be few,
then many once again.
And let your change of light
instruct the world.
Let you and all the nations
share one light, and pass it
back and forth. If you cooperate
with them and they with you,
someday your inner light
shall be restored,
and you'll return from wandering,
and will be One!"[4]

The Succah and the Huppah

By Debra Cash

We live in the world; most of us live in houses and apartment buildings, near busy streets. But there are two temporary structures that we build in our lifetimes. One is the succah, the desert booth. The other is the huppah, the wedding canopy.

Every year, the succah reminds us that once we had no permanent place, no land where we could sow and expect to reap at the end of a long growing season. It reminds us that once we were wanderers in the wilderness, and we longed for a home. We talk about how easily the succah collapses. It has firm walls, so that we can almost pretend that it is real, but we lay tree branches across the roof for thatch, tie paper birds and gourds from the rafters, and count the stars through the leaves.

The huppah is different. Who could mistake it for a real house? Its walls are nonexistent. The roof is flimsy. Wind can blow through the huppah. The rain is welcome. The couple who stand under its shelter must leave it to look up and see the stars.

But it is the huppah that we take for our home when we are promising each other everything. It is raised, for most of us, once in a lifetime. It is not permanent. But it is the promise of a home.

Its openness pledges that there will be no secrets. Friends and family stand at the corners, weighing the fragile structure down. The roof is often a tallit so that the bride and groom are covered by holiness and the memory of commandments.

The huppah does not promise that love or hope or pledges will keep out weather or catastrophe. But its few lines are a sketch for what might be.

The man and woman have left the desert of their loneliness. They have come from far away to be together. The flimsiness of the huppah reminds them that the only thing that is real about a home is the people in it who love and choose to be together, to be a family. The only anchor that they will have will be holding onto each others' hands.

The huppah is the house of promises. It is the home of hope.[5]

Eshet Chayil
A New Version
BY SUSAN GROSSMAN

*A good wife who can find her
she is worth far more than rubies
she brings good and not harm
all the days of her life
she girds herself with strength
and finds her trades profitable
wise counsel is on her tongue
and her home never suffers for warmth
she stretches her hands to the poor
reaches her arms to the needy
all her friends praise her
her family blesses her
she is known at the gates
as she sits with the elders
dignity, honor are her garb
she smiles at the future.*

A good man who can find him
he is worth far more than rubies
all who trust in him
never lack for gain
he shares the household duties
and sets a goodly example
he seeks a satisfying job
and braces his arms for work
he opens his mouth with wisdom
he speaks with love and kindness
his justice brings him praises
he raises the poor, lowers the haughty.

These two indeed do worthily
true leaders in Zion
give them their due credit
let their works praise them at the gates.[6]

The Song of Songs: A Translation from the Song of Songs

BY MARCIA FALK

VII

In sandy earth or deep
In valley soil
I grow, a wildflower thriving
On your love.

Narcissus in the brambles,
Brightest flower—
I choose you from all others
For my love.

Sweet fruit tree growing wild
Within the thickets—
I blossom in your shade
And taste your love.[7]

Brit Ahuvim:
A Reformulation of the Jewish Wedding*

Brit Ahuvim is not an alternative version of the Jewish wedding, but an altogether different instrument for creating marriages. Even the most apparently egalitarian Jewish wedding is grounded in ancient property law, which makes the wedding into a symbolic purchase of the bride by the groom through the ritual of *kinyan*. While liberal Jewish weddings make it appear that the gesture is mutual (with a double-ring ceremony), *kinyan* within *kiddushin* remains a unilateral act of acquisition by the groom. In Brit Ahuvim, however, neither partner acquires the other even symbolically; instead, both members of the couple acquire a partnership in which power is shared equally.

With Brit Ahuvim, Professor Rachel Adler makes the radical suggestion that liberal Jews take Jewish law *halakhah* seriously enough to understand and ultimately reject its view of marriage. Her book, *Engendering Judaism*, contains Hebrew texts of the documents cited here, which appear with permission.

The Brit Ahuvim documents and ceremony below offer an entirely different basis for marriage rooted in the Jewish laws that govern partnership agreements. These are bilateral agreements, with each partner ac-

---

* This appendix is based on the work of Rachel Adler in her book *Engendering Judaism: An Inclusive Theology and Ethics* (Beacon Press, 1998), which fully explains how Brit Ahuvim expresses a fundamental rethinking of *halakhah* (Jewish law). As Adler explains, *halakhah* (from the word meaning "to walk" or "to go") "translates the stories and values of Judaism into ongoing action. That makes it an integral component not merely of Orthodoxy, but of any kind of Judaism."

cepting obligations and responsibilities for maintaining the relationship. Thus, in a Brit Ahuvim ceremony, there is no declaration, "Behold you are sanctified to me with this ring according to the laws of Moses and Israel," nor is there a *ketubah*. Instead, the couple forms a partnership that they ratify with a custom described in the Talmud. This symbolic ratification was called *l'hatil b'kis*, literally "to put into one pouch," because the ancient gesture for pooling resources was for each partner to put a sum into one pouch and lift it up together.

A contract between two adults, Brit Ahuvim is fully enacted by its partners by signing their *brit* (covenant) document and does not require rabbinic sanction. (To be recognized by the state, however, it would require an officiant who is legally empowered to sign a marriage license.)

The Brit Ahuvim ritual and documents that follow can be modified to suit each couple's situation and requirements; they have been used by heterosexual, gay, and lesbian couples. And while they do represent a truly radical reformulation, the rituals and language satisfy the need for continuity as well as imagination by blending time-honored customs and language with new ideas.

Outline of a Brit Ahuvim Ceremony

1. *Mi adir al ha-kol*, traditional invocation

2. Officiant's speech

3. Blessing over wine

4. Reading the *brit* document in Hebrew and English

5. *Kinyan:* acquisition of the partnership by placing symbols of pooled resources in a bag and jointly lifting it. These can be objects—including rings if the couple wishes—that represent what each person brings to the relationship. After explaining the contents, the couple

recites a blessing. (For example, "Blessed are you . . . who remembers your covenant and is faithful to your covenant and keeps your word.") If there are rings in the bag, the couple would them remove them and put them on.

6. *Sheva Brachot*

7. Shattering of the glass

8. *Yihud.*

Brit Ahuvim Lovers Covenant

On ___ (day of the week) the ___ (day) of _____ (month), 57 ___ , according to Jewish reckoning, ___ month ___ day ___ year, according to secular reckoning in the city of _____, _____ (state) _____ (nation) _____ (Hebrew name) daughter/son of _____ and _____ whose surname is _____, and _____ (Hebrew name) daughter/son of _____ and _____ whose surname is _____ confirm in the presence of witnesses a lovers' covenant between them and declare a partnership to establish a household among the people of Israel.

The agreement into which _____ and _____ are entering is a holy covenant like the ancient covenants of our people, made in faithfulness and peace to stand forever. It is a covenant of protection and hope like the covenant God swore to Noah and his descendants, saying "When the bow is in the clouds, I will see it and remember the everlasting covenant between God and all living creatures, all flesh that is on earth. That," God said to Noah, "shall be the sign of the covenant that I have established between me and all flesh." (Genesis 9:16–17)

It is a covenant of distinction, like the covenant God made with Israel, saying, "You shall be My people I shall be your God." (Jeremiah 30:22)

It is a covenant of devotion, joining hearts like the covenant David and Jonathan made, as it is said, "And Jonathan's soul was bound up with the soul of David. Jonathan made a covenant with David because he loved him as himself." (1 Samuel 18:1—3)

It is a covenant of mutual lovingkindness like the wedding covenant between God and Zion, as it is said, "I will espouse you forever. I will espouse you with righteousness and justice and lovingkindness and compassion. I will espouse you in faithfulness and you shall know God." (Hosea 2:19—20)

Provisions of the Covenant

The following are the provisions of the lovers' covenant in which _____ (Hebrew name) daughter/son of _____ and _____, and _____ (Hebrew name) daughter/son of _____ and _____ now enter:

1. _____ and _____ declare that they have chosen each other as companions as our rabbis teach: "_Get yourself a companion._ This teaches that a person should get a companion, to eat with, to drink with, to study Bible with, to study Mishnah with, to sleep with, to confide all one's secrets, secrets of Torah and secrets of worldly things." (_Avot D'Rabbi Natan_ 8)

2. _____ and _____ declare that they are setting themselves apart for each other and will take no other lover.

3. _____ and _____ hereby assume all the rights and obligations that apply to family members: to attend, care and provide for one another [and for any children with which they may be blessed] [and for _____, _____ and _____, child/children of _____.]

4. _____ and _____ commit themselves to a life of kindness and righteousness as a Jewish family and to work together toward the communal task of mending the world.

5. _____ and _____ pledge that one will help the other at the time of dying, by carrying out the last rational request of the dying partner, protecting him/her from indignity or abandonment and by tender, faithful presence with the beloved until the end, fulfilling what has

been written: "Set me as seal upon your arm, for love is stronger than death." (Song of Songs, 8:6)

To this covenant we affix our signatures.

The partners:

_____

_____

Witnessed this day the ___ day of Parashat _____, _____ (Hebrew date)

The Witnesses:

_____

_____

Betrothal/ *Tenaim*

Prenuptial agreements are nothing new: Jewish law and custom provide for a document and a ceremony spelling out the obligations and terms—and dreams—of a couple planning to wed. The traditional *tenaim* text below is essentially a contract agreeing to a marriage. The prenuptial agreement that follows is a promise to abide by Jewish law regarding divorce.

Finally, the "Prayer on the Day of Betrothal," suggests the poetry and spiritual longing inherent in the most important human pledge and promise. This poem might be recited on the occasion of a *tenaim* celebration, or it can be the introduction to a series of written "conditions" of marriage agreed to by the couple—from very practical matters (finances, domicile), to promises from the heart (cherishing one another's children and parents).

Traditional *Tenaim* Text

To a Good Fortune

May it come up and sprout forth like a green garden whoso finds a wife finds a great good, and obtains favor of the good Lord who ratifies this union

May He who predestinates, bestow a good name and future to the provisions embodied in this agreement, which were agreed upon by the two parties hereto, that is, as party of the first part, Mr. _____ who represents the groom, Mr. _____, and as party of the second part, Mr. _____ who represents the bride Miss _____ .

Firstly: That the above named groom agrees to take himself as wife the above named bride, through *huppah* and betrothal, in accordance with the Laws of Moses and Israel; that they will neither abstract nor conceal from one another any property whatsoever, but they shall equally have power over their property, pursuant to the established custom.

The above named groom obligates himself to present the bride with gifts according to custom.

The above named bride obligates herself to give as her dowry the sum of _____ in cash, and clothes, pillows and linens, as is the custom.

The wedding will take place, if the Almighty so wills it, on the ___ day of _____ in the year _____ or sooner than such date if both parties agree thereto.

A fine is to be paid, by the party breaking this agreement, to the other party, in the fixed sum of _____ and also in accordance with the laws of the land.

All of the forgoing was done with perfect understanding and due deliberation, and by means of the most effective method, in accordance with the ordinances of the sages, of blessed memory, and in accordance with the laws of the land; by means of striking hands, by solemn promises, by true affirmation, by handing over an object (from one contracting party to another), to take effect immediately; and this is not to be regarded as a mere forfeiture without consideration, or as a mere formula or document. We have followed the legal formality of a symbolic delivery (*kinyan*), by handing over an object, between the groom and the bride and their representatives, by using a garment legally fit for the purpose, to validate all that is stated above.

And Everything Is Valid and Confirmed

Attested to _____ groom
Attested to _____ bride
Attested to _____ witness
Attested to _____ witness

Ritual Prenuptial Agreement

In the event that the covenant of marriage entered into on the ____ day of
_____, 20___, by _____ and _____, shall be terminated
by the civil authorities, then _____ and _____ shall voluntarily and promptly upon demand by either of the parties present themselves at a mutually convenient time and place to terminate the marriage
and release each other from the covenant of marriage in accordance with
Jewish law and custom.

This agreement is recognized as a material inducement to the marriage by the parties hereto. Failure of either of the parties to perform the
obligations hereunder if requested to do so by the other party shall ren-
der him or her libel for all costs, including attorneys' fees, reasonably in-
curred by the requesting party to secure his or her performance.

Entered into this ____ day of _____ 20___

Signed by husband, wife and two witnesses

Prayer on the Day of Betrothal

All Merciful God!
God of Love!
You have created for the soul another soul
To sympathize with.
For the heart another heart
To beat like it.

Grant that I have chosen a loving, noble being.
Bless my choice, Oh God,
So that there may proceed from the union of our hearts and minds
joys without number.[8]

Debra Cash

Jewish Wedding Artists

Elaine Adler (*ketubot*, invitations)
3 Sunny Knoll Terrace
Lexington, MA 02421
781-861-9679

Gad Almaliah (*ketubot*)
208 Milton Street
Dedham, MA 02026
800-783-0903
www.thedesignlabboston.com

Mickie Caspi (*ketubot*)
Caspi Cards & Art
P.O. Box 60022
Newtonville, MA 02460
800-KETUBOT/538-8268
www.caspicards.com

Peggy Davis (invitations, *ketubot*)
389 Adamsville Road
Colrain, MA 01340
413-624-3204
www.HebrewLettering.com

Amy Fagin (*ketubot*)
Twentieth Century Illuminations
P.O. Box 53
Athol, MA 01331
978-544-2247
www.20thcenturyilluminations.com

Jonathan Kremer (*ketubot*,
invitation design)
888-664-9625
www.kremerdesigns.com/kremer

Susan Leviton (*ketubot*,
invitations)
3417 N. 4th Street
Harrisburg, PA 17110
717-236-0231
gorelev@aol.com

Gloria Nelson (wedding cups)
Ceremonial Porcelains
7626 Sherwood Road
Philadelphia, PA 19151

Jeanette Kuvin Oren (*huppot*,
ketubot, "*simcha* chairs")
29 Dales Drive
Woodbridge, CT 06525
www.kuvinoren.com

Betsy Platkin Teutsch (*ketubot*)
629 West Cleveden Street
Philadelphia, PA 19119-3651
Bpteutsch@aol.com

NOTES

Introduction

1. Rabbi Harold Schulweis, "Blessed Are Our Differences," *Moment* magazine, Vol. 8, No. 8 (Sept. 1983/Tishrei 5744).

PART ONE: MAKING THE TRADITION YOUR OWN

1. Rabbi Maurice Lamm, *The Jewish Way in Love and Marriage* (San Francisco: Harper & Row, 1980), pp. 128–29 (Yevamot 63b).
2. Philip and Hanna Goodman, *The Jewish Marriage Anthology* (Philadelphia: Jewish Publication Society of America, 1965), p. 44 (Zohar 1:89a).
3. Lawrence Kushner, *The River of Light, Spirituality, Judaism and the Evolution of Consciousness* (San Francisco: Harper & Row, 1981), p. xii.
4. My adaptation of the story from *Pirke de Rabbi Eliezer,* trans. Gerald Friedlander (New York: Sepher-Hermon Press), p. 88, and Goodman, p. 34.
5. Goodman, p. 24 (Babylonian Talmud, Sotah 2a).
6. Goodman, p. 37 (Genesis Rabba, 68:4).
7. Lamm, p. 119.
8. Goodman, p. 30 (Baba Metzia 59a).
9. Ibid., p. 27 (Kiddushin 29b–30a).
10. For a thoughtful critique of traditional law and thought about Jewish marriage and weddings, see *"Brit Ahuvim:* A Marriage Between Subjects," in *Engendering Judaism: An Inclusive Theology and Ethics* by Rachel Adler (Boston: Beacon Press, 1998), pp. 169–209.
11. An interesting discussion of family conflict is found in Rabbi Edwin H. Friedman's article, "Systems and Ceremonies: A Family View of

Rites of Passage," from *The Family Life Cycle: A Framework for Family Therapy,* Monica McGoldrick and Elizabeth Carter, eds. (New York: Gardiner Press, 1980), pp. 429–52.

12. Friedman, "Systems and Ceremonies."

13. According to one estimate, one in every 37 American Jews was not born Jewish. For a complete discussion of converts and conversion, see Anita Diamant, *Choosing a Jewish Life: A Handbook for People Converting to Judaism and for their Family and Friends* (New York, Schocken Books, 1997).

14. Although it is increasingly common for liberal rabbis to require *mikvah, milah* or *hatafat dam brit* (drawing one drop of blood from an already-circumcised male), and/or *bet din,* not all do so.

15. Brenda Forster and Rabbi Joseph Tabachnik, *Jews by Choice: A Study of Converts to Reform and Conservative Judaism* (Hoboken, N.J.: KTAV, 1991), p. 49.

16. This tends to happen with the discovery that one wishes to have one's own death marked by Jewish burial, funeral, and mourning rites.

17. The Conservative rabbinate is on record as supporting "full civil liberty for gays and lesbians" and welcome for gay and lesbian Jews to Conservative congregations. However, as of March 1992, The Conservative Movement's Committee on Jewish Law and Standards ruled against officiation at same-sex ceremonies. For an eloquent dissent see Rabbi Elliot N. Dorf, *Matters of Life and Death: A Jewish Approach to Modern Medical Ethics* (Jewish Publication Society, 1998), pp. 139–151. Unlike the Reform and Reconstructionist movements, the Conservative movement does not ordain openly gay or lesbian rabbis or invest gay or lesbian cantors.

18. Hundreds of legal and economic protections available to heterosexual couples are denied to gay and lesbian couples. Even when there is a legal domestic partnership in place, the benefits to the partner are taxable where they are not for married couples. For information about the status of marriage and partnership law around the United

States, contact LAMBDA, Legal Defense and Education Fund, 120 Wall Street, Suite 1500, New York, NY 10005-3904, 212-809-8585. www.lambdalegal.org.

19. For a helpful resource see *A Legal Guide for Lesbian and Gay Couples,* Hayden Curry, ed. (Nolo Publications, 1999), www.nolo.com.

20. For more information, see *Points to Consider in Counseling Same-sex Couples for Marriage/Commitment Ceremonies.* C/O Aleph, 7318 Germantown Avenue, Philadelphia, PA 19119.

21. The late 1990s saw publication of several books about ceremonies (secular, Christian, Jewish, interfaith, etc.) for gay and lesbian couples, including: *Ceremonies of the Heart: Celebrating Lesbian Unions* by Becky Butler (Seal Press, 1997); *Recognizing Ourselves: Ceremonies of Lesbian and Gay Commitment* by Ellen Levin (Columbia University Press, 1998). Check the Internet for new titles.

22. Rabbi Barbara Penzner, based on an idea by Deborah Eisenbach-Budner.

23. Ariella Keysar, et al., Highlights of the Counsel of Jewish Federations 1990 National Jewish Population Survey (New York: Counsel of Jewish Federations, 1990), p. 14.

24. Kushner, op. cit.

25. See Paul Cowan with Rachel Cowan, *Mixed Blessings: Overcoming the Stumbling Blocks in an Interfaith Marriage* (Penguin, 1989), and Judy Petsonk and Jim Remsen, *The Intermarriage Handbook: A Guide for Jews and Christians* (Quill, 1991).

PART TWO: WAYS AND MEANS

1. Rabbi Maurice Lamm, *The Jewish Way in Love and Marriage* (San Francisco: Harper & Row, 1981), p. 179.

2. Abraham Joshua Heschel, *The Sabbath: Its Meaning for Modern Man* (New York: Farrar, Straus & Giroux, 1981), p. 8.

3. Ibid.

4. Philip and Hanna Goodman, *The Jewish Marriage Anthology*

(Philadelphia: Jewish Publication Society of America, 1965), p. 172.

5. Richard Siegel, Sharon Strassfeld, and Michael Strassfeld, *The First Jewish Catalog* (Philadelphia: Jewish Publication Society, 1973), p. 57.

6. Lamm, p. 221.

7. Lamm, p. 222.

8. Lamm, p. 198.

9. Goodman, p. 90.

10. Ibid.

11. Moses Gaster, *The Ketubah* (published 1924; reprinted New York: Sepher-Hermon Press, 1974), p. 48.

12. Ibid., p. 20.

13. I heard the words *brit ketubah* from Rabbi Max Ticktin of Washington, D.C.

14. Best-known among these divorce codicils is the Lieberman clause, named for its author, Rabbi Saul Lieberman, affirmed by the Conservative movement Joint Law Conference, and required by most Conservative rabbis: "And in solemn assent to their mutual responsibilities of love, the bridegroom and bride have declared: As evidence of our desire to enable each other to live in accordance with the Jewish Law of Marriage throughout our lifetime, we, the bride and bridegroom, attach our signatures to this *ketubah* and hereby agree to recognize the *Beth Din* of the Rabbinical Assembly of America or its duly appointed representatives as having authority to counsel us in the light of Jewish tradition, which requires husband and wife to give each other complete love and devotion and to summon either party at the request of the other in order to enable the party so requesting to live in accordance with the standards of the Jewish Law of Marriage throughout his or her lifetime. We authorize the *Beth Din* to impose such terms of compensation as it may see fit for failure to respond to its summons or to carry out its decisions." Published in:

Isaac Klein, *A Guide to Jewish Religious Practice,* The Jewish Theological Seminary of America (New York, 1979), p. 393.

15. Zalman Schachter-Shalomi with Donald Gropman, *The First Step* (New York: Bantam Books, 1983), p. 40.

16. This is also commonly known as the *"Jewish Catalog* Ketubah," where it appeared in 1973.

17. The "side document," also written by Debra Cash and David Fillingham, was signed along with their *ketubah* and functions as an alternative to the Lieberman clause, noted above:

On ___, 20__ which corresponds to _____ 57 _____, _____ (groom's name) and _____ (bride's name) entered into a covenant of marriage. With God as our help, we will strive to build a loving and harmonious life together. Separately and together, we will seek out the guidance of friends, teachers and counselors in situations that one or both of us believe endangers the continuation of our bond.

However, if either of us chooses to dissolve this marriage, neither of us will act as a recalcitrant spouse (*mored/moredet*). We hereby agree to the process of convening a *bet hesed* in order to end this relationship in our Jewish community as well as under civil procedures in the nation where we live.

Following the filing of a civil divorce petition and under all circumstances, before the finalization of a civil court decree, we will convene a panel of three wise persons. _____ (groom) and _____ (bride) will each choose one representative as his or her advocate. The two representatives so chosen will select a third person. Members of the panel should be familiar with the general issues of Jewish law and the mores of the community in which we live. Although it is preferred that members of the *bet hesed* be rabbis or Judaic scholars, this will not be required.

Members of the *bet hesed* may meet as many times as they feel is necessary among themselves or with the divorcing couple. However, members of the *bet hesed* will themselves be required to commit to an expeditious process. All payment for the services of the *bet hesed* will be paid from funds jointly held.

We will abide by the decision of this *bet hesed* in enacting any solemn ritual or ceremony of divorce that is defined by the members of the panel within the bounds of civil law. In addition, we will create a document formalizing our Jewish divorce that will be available for inspection by family members, potential spouses, and by lawyers or authorities involved in our civil divorce. All issues associated with the division of our property will be handled by the civil courts in accordance with our prenuptial contract and civil divorce decree.

By entering into the process of a *bet hesed*, we pledge that neither will create an impediment to the other's Jewish remarriage. Specifically, we pledge that under the guidance of a *bet hesed*, if one of us requires a formal *get* from the other, in accordance with any denomination of the Jewish world that the requester identifies, the other will not be recalcitrant and will participate in person or by a proxy acceptable under the norms of that denomination's practice.

So may we work for a time when no marriage among the children of Israel is bound by chains. All of this is valid and binding. (Signature of bride, groom and two witnesses.)

Thanks to Debra Cash and David Fillingham for permission to reprint.

18. Goodman, p. 97.
19. Rabbi Aryeh Kaplan, *Made in Heaven* (New York: Moznaim Publishing Co., 1983), p. 145.
20. Ellen Deutch Quint, "Huppah Whoopee," *The Jewish Women's Resource Center Newsletter*, vol. II, no. 2, fall 1980, pp. 8–9. National Council of Jewish Women, New York Section.

21. Goodman, p. 28.
22. Hayyim Schauss, *The Lifetime of a Jew* (New York: Union of American Hebrew Congregations, 1950), pp. 187–88.
23. Rabbi Lawrence Kushner.
24. The Internet is a wonderful resource for Jewish music. Try keywords "klezmer," "Jewish music," and "Jewish wedding music" for interesting sites. A few excellent sites include: www.kleszmershack.com, which contains listings for musicians, musical organizations, reviews, as well as books and recordings, and links to all kinds of Jewish musical sites; www.jewishmusic.com sells compact disks, music books, and other resources; www.yiddishmusic.com has sheet music and recordings; www.hatikvahmusic.com offers a good selection of CDs.
25. Rabbi Burt Jacobson, "Jewish Wedding Workbook," p. 60.
26. Lamm, p. 214.
27. Kaplan, *Made in Heaven*, p. 161. The seven relatives that become forbidden to the groom are: the bride's mother, her daughter, her sister, her mother's mother, her father's mother, her son's daughter, and her daughter's daughter.
28. See n. 26, above.
29. Samson Raphael Hirsch, *Horeb* (London: Soncino Press, 1973), p. 533.
30. Lamm, p. 168.
31. Samuel H. Dresner, *The Jewish Dietary Laws* (New York: Burning Bush Press, 1955), p. 19.
32. For more information about *kashrut*, see: *The Jewish Dietary Laws*, ibid.; Rabbi Hayim Halevy Donin, *To Be a Jew* (New York: Basic Books, 1972), pp. 97–120; Anita Diamant, *Living a Jewish Life* (New York: HarperCollins, 1991), pp. 95–107.
33. Rabbi Eugene Borowitz.
34. Goodman, pp. 105–111.
35. Schauss, p. 186.
36. See n. 24

37. Hayyim Schneid, *Marriage* (Jerusalem: Keter Books, 1973), pp. 42–43.

PART THREE: CELEBRATIONS AND RITUALS

1. Samson Raphael Hirsch, *Horeb* (London: Soncino Press, 1962), p. 533.
2. This is a description of the *tenaim* ceremony by and for Barbara Rosman Penzner and Brian Penzner Rosman.
3. For more information and ideas about making *tallesim* and other gifts, see *The First Jewish Catalog* (Philadelphia: Jewish Publication Society, 1973), and *The New Jewish Yellow Pages* (Englewood, N.J.: SBS Publishing Inc., 1980).
4. The *Mi She'beirakh* is a "prayer for all occasions," according to Rabbi Hayim Halevy Donin, *To Pray as a Jew* (New York: Basic Books, 1980), p. 251. It may be said on behalf of a sick person or to wish well to a bar mitzvah or for the health of a newborn child and his/her mother. It is also the setting for naming girl children in the synagogue. The *Mi She'beirakh* on behalf of a couple about to be married invokes God's blessing on the bride and groom, with wishes for their happiness and success in creating a Jewish home.
5. *Siddur Chaveirim Kol Yisraeil.* For information about this prayer book: Progressive Chavurah/Siddur Committee, c/o David Merfeld, 21 Merchants Row, Suite 5, Boston, MA 02109. www.mitz.net/chavurah/siddur.
6. For a thoughtful examination of *mikvah* and the laws of *taharat hamishpacha* see the essay by Rachel Adler in *The Jewish Woman,* ed. Elizabeth Koltun (New York: Schocken Books, 1976).
7. Since biblical times Jews have immersed themselves in *mikvaot* in order to transform *tumah* into *taharah,* terms generally translated, respectively, as "unclean" and "pure." However, some people believe that this translation has led to a misunderstanding of the meaning of *mikvah.*

When the Temple stood in Jerusalem, the High Priest entered the Holy of Holies only once a year, on Yom Kippur. When he emerged from the innermost sanctuary he had to immerse himself in a *mikvah* before putting on his robes. Clearly, this encounter with the holy did not make him "unclean"; however, in coming so close to the Source of power, he became *tamay*. The preparation of corpses for burial, which is considered a great *mitzvah*, also renders one *tamay;* so does childbirth.

Although the Bible implies that the cycle of *tumah/taharah* was a way for everyone to experience the terrifying/mysterious/holy processes of death and rebirth, after the destruction of the Temple, most of the laws of *tumah* that applied to men were discarded. The laws regarding *niddah* became codified into *taharat hamishpacha* (the purity of the family), and as Rachel Adler writes in *The Jewish Woman, tamay* "became a special condition afflicting only women."

8. Rabbi Aryeh Kaplan, *Waters of Eden: The Mystery of the Mikvah* (New York: National Conference of Synagogue Youth/Union of Orthodox Jewish Congregations, 1976), p. 35.

9. Penina Adelman, *Miriam's Well: Rituals for Jewish Women Around the Year* (Fresh Meadows, NY: Biblio Press) pp. 98–103.

10. Richard Siegel and Carl Rheins, eds. *The Jewish Almanac* (New York: Bantam Books, 1980), pp. 541–42.

11. These prayers come from a *mikvah* celebration entitled "The Voice of God Echoes Across the Waters," which may be obtained for the cost of copying and postage from the Creative Liturgy Library of the Reconstructionist Rabbinical College, Church Road and Greenwood Avenue, Wyncote, PA 19095.

12. This poem, written by Gerald Dicker, appears in *Vehater Libeynu* (Purify Our Hearts), *siddur* of Congregation Beth El of the Sudbury River Valley, Sudbury, MA (1980), p. 114.

13. From "A Jewish Wedding Workbook," by Rabbi Burt Jacobson.

14. Translation by Mark Frydenberg from Siddur Chaveirim Kol Yisraeil, op. cit.

15. Translation by Debra Cash.

16. From a wedding booklet written by Rabbi William Feyer, Atlanta, Georgia.

17. From a wedding service written by Rabbi Burt Jacobson.

18. Rabbi Wolli Kaelter of Long Beach, CA. Privately printed and distributed.

19. The addition of "as my wife" (and also "as my husband") in the English translation of the *haray aht* reflects the differentiation of gender apparent in Hebrew nouns.

20. Rabbi Aryeh Kaplan, *Made in Heaven* (New York: Moznaim Publishing Co., 1983), p. 177.

21. These arrangements were once considered crucial because the marriage could not be legally consummated unless the *ketubah* was in the bride's possession.

22. Translations in this section are by Rachel Adler, op. cit., page 181.

23. *Rabbi's Manual of the Reconstructionist Rabbinical Association*© 1997, Reconstructionist Rabbinical Association. The chapter called "*Berit Ahavah,* which is devoted to helping gay and lesbian couples fashion Jewish commitment ceremonies/weddings. The Hebrew reflects the changes in the English, as seen here, with gender references appropriate for either two men or two women.

24. © Joel Rosenberg, July 1, 1979, in honor of the wedding of Richard A., and Jeanne B. Siegel. Printed with permission.

25. The Talmud was completed by the fifth century, C.E.

26. Goodman, p. 28.

27. Lamm, p. 229.

28. Daniel I. Leifer, "On Writing New Ketubot," *The Jewish Woman,* Elizabeth Koltun, ed. (New York: Schocken Books, 1976) pp. 50–61.

29. Information regarding *sheva shevachot* comes from the files of the Jewish Women's Resource Center, NCJW, 9 East 69th Street, New York, NY 10021. Particularly useful were the two *sheva shevachot*

ceremonies compiled by Serena Wieder and Beverly Worthman (Winter 1978).

30. This translation of *birkat hamazon* is adapted from *Vetaher Libeynu* (Purify Our Hearts), *siddur* of Congregation Beth El of the Sudbury River Valley. Other sources include a translation by Rabbi Zalman Schachter-Shalomi, and the discussion of *birkat hamazon* in Donin, *To Pray as a Jew,* pp. 287–301.

PART FOUR: CREATING A JEWISH HOME

1. *Vetaher Libeynu* (Purify Our Hearts), *siddur* of Congregation Beth El of the Sudbury River Valley, Sudbury, MA (1980), p. 8.
2. From a poem by Debra Cash that appears on pages 228–29.
3. From a *ketubah* by Rabbi Gustav Buchdahl, Rabbi Lawrence Kushner, and Rabbi Bernard H. Mehlman.
4. Gittin 90b.
5. National resources include:
   Beth Din of America
   305 Seventh Avenue, 12th floor
   New York, NY 10001
   www.bethdin.org
     See also Rabbi Kenneth Auman and Rabbi Basil Herring, eds., *The Prenuptial Agreement: Halakhic, Legal, and Pastoral Concerns* (New York: Jason Aronson and the Orthodox Caucus, 1995).
6. Bracha Osofsky, "Progress on the Get Problem," *Lilith,* no. 10 (Winter 1982–83), pp. 4–5.
7. Text by Rabbis Harold Bloom and Lawrence Kushner.
8. Rabbi Leigh Lerner, "Restore the Get," *Reform Judaism* magazine, spring 2000, p. 58. This issue contains several articles about how Reform Jews are reclaiming and reshaping traditional Jewish divorce practices.
9. For a sample divorce ritual and a fuller discussion of the subject, see

Rabbi Debra Orenstein, ed., "Divorce," *Lifecycles: Jewish Women on Life Passages & Personal Milestones* (Woodstock, VT: Jewish Lights Publishing, 1994), pp. 185–210.

APPENDICES

The Wedding Poems

1. © Joel Rosenberg, June 19, 1977, in honor of the wedding of Linda and William Novak.
2. © Joel Rosenberg, January 14, 1980, in honor of the wedding of Woshe Walkdocks and Anne Pomerantz.
3. © Joel Rosenberg, June 14, 1981, in honor of the wedding of Benjie Ellen Schiller and Les Bronstein.
4. © Joel Rosenberg, 1991, in honor of the wedding of Lisa Fried and Mark Snyderman.
5. © Debra Cash, June 6, 1982, for the sheva b'rachot of Yehuda Bodenstein Avniel and Sara Reva Horowitz.
6. © Rabbi Susan Grossman, 1980.
7. © Marcia Lee Falk, *The Song of Songs: Love Poems from the Bible*, (HarperCollins, 1990). To purchase copies of this and her other works: www.marciafalk.com
8. Adapted from *Devotions for the Daughters of Israel*, by Marcus Heinrich Bresslau, 1852, London. Thanks to Ruth Abusch-Magder for her archival assistance.

GLOSSARY

AGUNAH   Literally, "a chained woman": one whose marriage has not been terminated according to Jewish law and who is thus prohibited from remarrying

ALEPH-BET   Name of the Hebrew alphabet; also, its first two letters

ALIYAH   Literally, "to go up": to be called to the Torah. Also, "making *aliyah*" refers to moving to the land of Israel

ARAMAIC   Semitic language closely related to Hebrew, the lingua franca of the Middle East. The Talmud was written in Aramaic, as are traditional legal documents, including *ketubah, tenaim,* and *get*

ASHKENAZIC   Jews and Jewish culture of Eastern and Central Europe

AUFRUF   Recognition of a groom and bride by calling them up to the Torah on the Shabbat immediately preceding a wedding

BAAL SHEM TOV   Israel ben Eliezer, founder of Hasidism, the eighteenth-century mystical revival movement

BADCHAN   Master of ceremonies at a wedding celebration

BARUCH ATA ADONAI ELOHEYNU MELECH HAOLAM   Words that begin Hebrew blessings, most commonly rendered in English as "Blessed art Thou, Lord our God, King of the Universe." This book contains many alternatives to that translation

B.C.E.   Before the Common Era. Jews avoid using the Christian designation B.C., which means "before Christ"

BEDEKEN   Ritual ceremony of veiling the bride before the wedding ceremony

BET DIN   Rabbinical court

BIMAH   Raised platform in the synagogue, dais

BRIS/BRIT   Covenant. *Bris* and *brit milah* refer to the covenant of circumcision

C.E.   Common Era. Jews avoid the designation A.D., which means "in the year of our Lord"

CHALLAH   Braided loaf of white bread, traditional for Shabbat and the holidays

CHOSSEN   Yiddish for "groom"; in Hebrew, *hatan*

CHOSSEN'S TISH   Literally, "groom's table": the name of the celebration for the groom and his friends prior to the wedding ceremony

CONSERVATIVE   Religious movement, developed in the United States during the twentieth century as a more traditional response to modernity than that offered by Reform

DAVEN   Pray

D'RASH   Religious insight, often on a text from the Torah

D'VAR TORAH   Literally, "words of Torah": an explication about a portion of the Torah

ERUSIN   Betrothal ceremony

FLEISHIG   Meat food, which, according to *kashrut,* may not be mixed with dairy products

FREILACH   Yiddish for "happy"; also, up-tempo songs

GET   Formal document of Jewish divorce

HALAKHAH   Jewish law

HASIDISM   Eighteenth-century mystical revival movement that stressed God's immanence in the world. The doctrine of *simcha,* joy, was expounded as a way of communing with God; *simcha* was expressed in singing, dancing, feasting, and rejoicing

HATAN   Hebrew for "groom"; in Yiddish, *chossen*

HAVDALAH   Hebrew for "separation": Saturday-evening ceremony that separates Shabbat from the rest of the week

HAVURAH   Literally, "fellowship": small, intimate participatory groups of Jews who meet for prayer, study, and celebration

HAZZAN   Cantor

HUPPAH   Wedding canopy

KADDISH   Mourner's prayer

KALLAH   Bride (Hebrew)

KASHRUT   System of laws that govern what and how Jews eat

KETUBAH   Marriage contract

KIDDUSHIN   Sanctification: a name for the betrothal ceremony; also, a term for the entire wedding ceremony

KITTEL   White robe sometimes worn by the groom under the canopy

KLEZMER   Jewish music

KOSHER   Permissible to be eaten according to the laws of *kashrut;* in general, proper or legitimate

MACHETUNIM   Relatives by marriage

MAVEN   An expert

MAZEL TOV   Literally, "Good luck," but in practice, "Congratulations!"

MENSCH   Person; an honorable, decent person

MESADER KIDDUSHIN   One who "orders" or leads the marriage ceremony

MEZUZAH   First two paragraphs of the Shema written on a parchment scroll and encased in a small container, to be affixed to the doorposts of a home

MILCHIG   Dairy foods, which, according to *kashrut,* may not be mixed with meat products

MIDRASH   Imaginative exposition of scripture

MIKVAH   Ritual bath

MINHAG   Custom

MINYAN   Group of at least ten adult Jews (for traditional Jews, ten men; for liberal Jews, men or women) that serves as the basic unit for community prayer

MISHEGAS   Foolishness

MITZVAH   Commandment; a good deed (pl. *mitzvot*)

MIZRACHI   Jews of the Middle East and North Africa

MOTZI   Blessing over bread recited before meals

NACHES   Special joy from the achievements of one's children

NIGGUN   Wordless melody

NISSUIN   Ceremony of the nuptials

ONEG SHABBAT   Literally, "Sabbath delight." In America it has become synonymous with the informal meal or snack that follows Friday-night services

ORTHODOX   Generally, strictly traditional. The Modern Orthodox movement developed in the nineteenth century in response to the Enlightenment and Reform Judaism.

PARASHA   Weekly Torah portion

RABBI   Teacher. "The rabbis" refers to the men who codified the Talmud

RECONSTRUCTIONIST   Religious movement, begun in the United States in the twentieth century by Mordecai Kaplan, that views Judaism as an evolving religious civilization

REFORM   Movement, begun in nineteenth-century Germany, that sought to reconcile Jewish tradition and thought with modernity and the Enlightenment

ROSH HODESH   First day of every lunar month; the New Moon, a semi-holiday

SCHMOOZ   Friendly chatter

SEPHARDIM   Jews from Spain, Portugal, and the Mediterranean

SHABBAT   Sabbath

SHADCHAN   Matchmaker

SHECHINAH   God's feminine attributes

SHEHEHIYANU   Prayer of thanksgiving for new blessings

SHEVA B'RACHOT   Seven marriage blessings; first recited under the canopy, and following meals for seven days when a *minyan* is present

SHIDDUCH   Marriage match

SHOFAR   Ram's horn, blown during the High Holidays

SHTETL   Small town, especially one inhabited by Ashkenazic Jews before the Holocaust

SHUL   Synagogue

SIDDUR   Daily and Shabbat prayer book

SIMCHA   Joy and the celebration of joy

SOFER   Ritual scribe

TAHARAT HAMISHPACHAH   Laws of family purity prescribing women's sexual availability and the use of *mikvah*

TALLIS or TALLIT   Prayer shawl

TALMUD   Encyclopedic compilation of rabbinic thought, lore, and law consisting of the Mishnah and Gemarah, completed around the fifth century, C.E.

TENAIM   Literally, "conditions": formal engagement contracts; also, the name of the celebration that attends the signing of the document

TORAH   First five books of the Hebrew Bible, portions of which are read every Shabbat

TSEDAKAH   Charity; righteous action toward the poor

YICHUD   "Seclusion": ten- or fifteen-minute period immediately following the marriage ceremony during which bride and groom are alone with each other

YIDDISH   Language spoken by Ashkenazic Jews; combination of early German and Hebrew

YIDDISHKEIT   Jewishness

ZOHAR   Literally, "splendor": thirteenth-century text of Jewish mysticism

INDEX

Page numbers in *italics* refer to illustrations.

ABOUT THE AUTHOR

Anita Diamant was born in 1951 in Brooklyn, New York, and grew up in Newark, New Jersey, and Denver, Colorado. She holds a bachelor's degree in Comparative Literature from Washington University and a master's degree in English from the State University of New York at Binghamton. Since 1975, she has made her home in the Boston area, where she lives with her husband and daughter.

A journalist for many years, her work has appeared in *The Boston Globe*, *Boston* magazine, *Hadassah*, *Parenting*, *Parents*, *Reform Judaism*, *Self*, and *Yankee* magazine, and online for jewishfamily.com.

She has written several guidebooks to contemporary Jewish life, including *How to Be a Jewish Parent*, *Saying Kaddish: How to Comfort the Dying, Bury the Dead and Mourn as a Jew*, *Choosing a Jewish Life: A Handbook for People Converting to Judaism and for Their Family and Friends*, *Living a Jewish Life: Jewish Traditions, Customs and Values for Today's Families*, *The New Jewish Baby Book*, and *Bible Baby Names*.

Anita Diamant is also the author of a best-selling novel, *The Red Tent*, which is based on the biblical story of Dinah, daughter of Jacob and Leah.